MY BANGS LOOK
GOOD
& OTHER LIES I TELL MYSELF

MY BANGS LOOK
GOOD
& OTHER LIES I TELL MYSELF

*THE TIRED SUPERGIRL'S
SEARCH FOR TRUTH*

SUSANNA FOTH AUGHTMON

Revell
a division of Baker Publishing Group
Grand Rapids, Michigan

Published by Revell
a division of Baker Publishing Group
P.O. Box 6287, Grand Rapids, MI 49516-6287
www.revellbooks.com

Printed in the United States of America

Library of Congress Cataloging-in-Publication Data
Aughtmon, Susanna Foth, 1970–
    My bangs look good and other lies I tell myself : the tired supergirl's search for truth / Susanna Foth Aughtmon.
        p.   cm.
    ISBN 978-0-8007-3418-3 (pbk.)
    1. Christian women—Religious life. 2. Aughtmon, Susanna Foth, 1970– I. Title.
    BV4527.A9 2010
    248.8'43—dc22   2009040242

10   11   12   13   14   15   16   7   6   5   4   3   2   1

For Scott—the one who holds my heart
and tells me the truth

contents

tired supergirl: tahy-rd soo-per-gurl.   noun. abbreviation: tsg. 1 : a follower of Jesus 2 : a seeker of grace, truth, a good pair of jeans, and a sassy haircut 3 : a woman caught living in the tension between the woman she is at present and the woman that God designed her to be 4 : a woman likely to be super or tired or super-tired 5 : a woman who may or may not feel comfortable wearing a unitard while trying to conquer the world 6 : a woman who may be felled by large amounts of laundry or a wicked chemistry final on occasion but is, by all accounts, a rock star, as she is loved by Jesus and listens for his voice in her life

acknowledgments

Super thanks to—

Scott. Who else would love me with such crazy hair? Thanks for always encouraging me to be more than I am.

Jack, Will, and Addison. Thanks for all those good hugs and kisses. I love being yours.

Mom, Dad, Dave, and Lola. Thanks for teaching Scott and me the truth when we were young. Love you.

The Clements, Moody, Foth, and Bondonno clans. Thanks for your truckloads of encouragement. You are the best.

The Pathway Crew. Thanks for walking on this journey with Scott and me.

Virda, Paula, Vanessa, Blenda, Jenn, Cheri, Sara, Darlene, Amie, and Lynette. Thanks for speaking truth to our boys. Your fingerprints are on their souls.

David and Kara. Thanks for investing in us, loving us, and always keeping it real . . . Big Bird style.

Lori. For your song that left me undone. Thanks for letting your words grace this book.

Wendy. I love having you on my side. I couldn't find a better agent. Not that I'm biased or anything.

Vicki. It is my joy to make you laugh. Thanks for being so much fun to work with.

The Revell team and Baker Publishing Group. The way you bring a dream to life is amazing. Thanks for using your gifts on behalf of a book about bangs, lies, and the truth of Jesus.

All the tired supergirls out there. Down with lies and bad hair! Thanks for reading. It is good to know we are in this together.

And mostly, super thanks to Jesus—for being the Truth.

introduction

Can we get a little truth up in here?

If this book is about truth, and it is, I suppose I must stick with telling stories that are true, no matter how very terrible they are. I have always been at odds with my baby-fine, straw-straight hair, and I have a secret fear that when I am elderly, I will be bald. But hopefully, I will also be delusional at that point, so I won't really care about my hair. I do care a bit about my hair at this point, however. I have had a few run-ins with my hair over the years that have given me pause: my too-short Dorothy Hamill wedge cut, my generic 1980s perm that burned my hair follicles, and my chocolate brown hair dyeing experience in which I ended up looking like a Russian spy (Susanka Aughtmonskova). But nothing prepared me for The Bang-tastrophe of 2008.

The day was highly irregular since, by some strange miracle, I had a small chunk of time without children. Seeing it as a perfect opportunity to go to the store, I grabbed my shoes from the closet and headed for the door. Then I caught sight of my bangs. Long. Limp. Lifeless. So I grabbed a pair of kitchen shears and *chop*, *chop*, I was ready to go. They seemed a little crooked, but nothing a little blow-dry wouldn't fix. I yelled good-bye to my husband, Scott, and raced out the door. At the store I tossed the items I needed in a basket and headed to the check stand. The boy who was bagging gave me a kind of sympathetic grin, which I thought was odd until I glanced down and noticed I had two different shoes on. Arriving back home, I went into Scott's office, pointing to my shoes.

"Look what I did! I wore two different shoes to the store," I explained. "I'm going to have to post a picture of this on my blog."

"Your hair!" was his horrified answer.

"What?"

"Go look at your hair."

"My hair? You mean my bangs? I just cut them. They don't look that bad, do they?"

I had my answer when Scott dropped to the floor in the fetal position.

I stepped into the bathroom and flipped on the light. Under the harsh glow of the bathroom lighting, I could not deny the truth. My bangs were hideous.

Starting at the far right corner of my forehead, my bangs proceeded upward at a steep incline to reveal one unkempt eyebrow in its entirety. Mid-forehead, a long, shapeless piece of bang hung down past the bridge of my nose. The bang line continued on haphazardly past the other eyebrow, coming to a forlorn stop near the left temple. Not only had I cut them very crooked, I had cut them very short, leaving only marginal room for a re-trim, lest I end up with a Frankenstein mini-bang look.

I forgot my mismatched shoes and joined Scott in the fetal position on the office floor. After an emergency re-trim that now revealed the other unkempt eyebrow in its full glory, Scott said, "They are still crooked."

At which point I screeched like a banshee, "I'm not going any higher!" I knew I looked a little bit like Jim Carrey in *Dumb and Dumber*, but what I longed for Scott to say was, "Sue, your hair is fine. You look great! No big deal."

But Scott is a truth teller, and the truth was that I had crooked, shorty-short bangs. I could pretend that my bangs looked good, but clearly the look from the bagger at the grocery store said they did not. I could pretend that the state of my bangs didn't matter to me, but that would be a lie, since I had to warn friends over the phone, "I did something wrong with my bangs," so they could prepare themselves mentally for what they were about to see. But because Scott loved me and knew I needed to face the reality of the situation, he told me the truth. I think he also told me the truth because my bangs traumatized him and he wanted to make sure that I never cut my bangs with kitchen shears again as long as we both shall live.

Sometimes we supergirls need to be told the truth—not just about our bangs but also about other lies that we believe. We need to know the truth about who Jesus is in our lives. We need to know the truth about what he thinks of us and what he requires of us. Because Jesus loves us, he tells us the truth. He is in the business of uniting the truth and our hearts. He is all about clarity and revelation and us owning our stuff, especially the good stuff.

We always seem to think that the truth is made up of all the awkward secrets we try to keep hidden away in the corners of our hearts. Our worst fear is that someone will share our secrets with the world at large, saying, "This girl has serious problems. And messes? Oh my word, she makes terrific messes of things. And lying? I don't want to shame her or anything, but it still reads 125 pounds on her driver's license. She hasn't seen that number in years. *Years.* Maybe even decades. Now that is the truth. Thanks for taking this time out of your day to find out who this person really is."

Now that would be horrific. It may be the truth, and if it is, you may want to either look into getting your driver's license changed or take up jogging. I am keeping the number on mine because I believe in miracles and that God may soon bring this number to pass in my life.

We often think of truth telling in the worst sense. But Jesus uses his truth in the healing sense of the word. I think if he told the truth about your life, it would go more like this:

This girl? I could squeeze her head right off. I love her to death. Seriously. She has had a lot of things going on. She's been hurt before. And sometimes she can't see her way clear past all the messes in her life. But the fantastic thing is, I died for her. I forgave her. And I took a peek inside her heart this morning, and you are not going to believe this, but she is full of kindness and wittiness, and you cannot believe the things she can do with yarn. Macramé is her gift. Oh, and did I tell you I love her to death? I did? Well, I had to say it again. That is the truth. Thanks for taking this time out of your day to find out who this person really is.

Okay, maybe you're not sure that you want people knowing about your gifting in the area of yarn. But what I'm trying to say is that Jesus wants to use truth to revolutionize the way you see yourself and the way you see him. He uses truth for good. Not for evil. Jesus is on our side, tired supergirls. He really is. And we will need his perfect truth on this journey, because we will be facing a nemesis who needs to be taken out in the strong name of the Lord. And I am not kidding.

This nemesis happens to be at direct odds with us tired supergirls knowing the truth. That would be the Liar. He is the granddaddy of all nemeses. Because he hates Jesus (and us, for that matter), he will never tell us the truth. He is looking to destroy us in any way he can. And tired supergirls, he is good at what he does. The Liar uses truth for evil. Yep. He uses only snippets of truth here and there, and he tries to use it to blind you to the whole truth. He would like to keep you in the dark about who God is and who you are designed to be. He is so good at spinning the truth that we supergirls tend to have a difficult time separating God's truth from his lies. The Liar is absolutely brilliant when it comes to using partial truth against us. He even tried it against Jesus.

Jesus was led into the desert by the Holy Spirit to be tempted for forty days and nights. He was parched. He was hungry. He was utterly alone—until the devil showed up. And that was not exactly the company Jesus was looking for. The devil tried to use Scripture to trip Jesus up. Scripture!

> Then the devil took him to the holy city, Jerusalem, to the highest point of the Temple, and said, "If you are the Son of God, jump off! For the Scriptures say, 'He will order his angels to protect you. And they will hold you up with their hands so you won't even hurt your foot on a stone.'"
> Jesus responded, "The Scriptures also say, 'You must not test the LORD your God.'"
>
> Matthew 4:5–7

Now let me just say, the devil really thinks a whole lot of himself and his abilities. As my husband Scott says, "He thinks he is all that and a bag of chips."

The Liar thought he was going to pull one over on Jesus. With Scripture. He was using God's own words against him. But the thing he was not counting on was that Jesus personified truth. He didn't just like the truth or try to tell the truth or have good feelings about the truth. Jesus was (and is) the Truth. At every point Jesus came into contact with lies or fabrications or chicanery of any kind, he was going to expose it for what it was. It was his nature. So when Satan challenged him with Scripture, Jesus turned it back on him and said, "You must not test the LORD your God" (Matt. 4:7).

That's kind of funny since that was exactly what Satan was doing. He was actually in the process of testing Jesus. Trying to find the weak place in him. Using odd bits of truth to try to take him down. But Jesus was so soaked in the truth, it wasn't working. And eventually Satan had to call it quits. I think being in the presence of all that truth made him really tired. And cranky.

So here we are. Our hearts are darkened with the semi-truthful lies told to us by the Liar. He has kept us in the dark for so long that we're not sure we really know what the truth looks like. But Jesus knows exactly what the truth looks like, and he is ready to flood all those dark corners with the light of his glorious truth, saying, "Ready?"

And the Liar is yelling, "Turn the lights off! My retinas are burning!"

We have a choice. We have the choice of saying, "Nope. I'm down with my lies. I like my half-truth darkened heart."

Or we can say to Jesus, "I want your truth—the truth about who I am (bad bangs and all) and the truth about who you are."

And having made your choice, you then hike up your high-heeled boots, flip your long, glorious, tired-supergirl hair (no Frankenstein haircut for you), and say, "*Bring. It. On!*"

And oh, tired supergirl, he will bring it. It is about to be brung. Brought. It's been brunged. You know what I'm saying.

So let's say this prayer together as we start this journey: *Jesus, may the light of your truth pierce our souls and heal us from the inside out. Show us the truth about who you are and who we are in you. Reshape our minds to think like yours. And keep us close. We love you. Amen.*

LIE #1
GOD IS OUT TO GET ME

From early on in life, I have had a sense that God knew where I was. This could be because as a pastor's kid, I was frequently told on when I was being naughty. A few hundred pairs of eyes never hurt when it came to keeping track of a rambunctious kid. I always wondered how my parents knew when I was up to no good. I figured they had a hotline to God. For some reason this never translated into a sense of safety for me, a sense that I could relax because God was keeping tabs on me. Instead, it smoldered and mushroomed into a Big-Brother-is-watching-me kind of fear, and I knew that I had better keep it all together. I knew that God knew what was going on in my life, and he was about to let my parents in on what was going on. God doesn't play. No, he doesn't. Think back for a moment on the prophets of Baal in the Old Testament. Remember them up on the hill? Disobeying God? Do you remember their demise? God smoked them. Yes, he did. That's enough biblical knowledge to keep any young girl on the straight and narrow.

My early spiritual life was based on the unhealthy fear that at any moment God could find me and take me out, which is funny and pretty sad since I never once heard my parents say anything to me about God chasing me down and striking me with bolts of lightning or about living out an eternity in a fiery pit of teeth-gnashing misery. But a couple years ago, I did hear my five-year-old, Jack, tell my three-year-old, Will, that he'd better ask Jesus into his heart or he was going straight to hell. So somehow, possibly by osmosis, five-year-olds in my family line have an inherent fear of being dealt a hard hand by God if we don't toe the line. I tried to explain to Jack that since Will was only three, he couldn't really understand what it means to ask Jesus into his heart. Jack looked at me like maybe I would also be visiting the lake of fire if I was going to try to keep Will out of the fold.

In my growing-up years I viewed myself as a "small sin" kind of sinner. By that I mean that I stayed far away from what I thought were the "big" sins. Sex. Drinking. Drugs. Stealing. I never once murdered anyone. In my mind, I was pretty good. I didn't rebel in high school. I was shocked to find out kids in my youth group went to parties and (be still my beating heart!) drank alcoholic beverages. To say I was a bit on the naïve side is putting it mildly. I almost passed out when I found out people at my Bible college, people who went to church and had no tattoos whatsoever, had sex before they were married. I felt great pity for them. I knew what was coming. At any moment God was going to get fed up, and these poor people were going to be swept away in a sea of God's fury like the Egyptian soldiers in the Red Sea. I lived a very simple theology. I was deathly afraid of God; therefore I tried to follow his rules so I wouldn't get squished. What a glorious faith I embraced! Think of all the joy and hope therein. Or maybe just nausea and cold sweats.

But it all came to a head in my junior year of college. I was at a pivotal point in my own faith. I was questioning whether or not I really wanted to obey God with my actions, with my words, with my life. And I chose to walk away.

Nine months later I found myself staring in the mirror, washing my face, and crying after making myself sick. I was on the fast track to becoming bulimic. And looking at myself I thought, "Either I am going to follow Jesus, or this is who I get to be—a person who wakes up in the morning and makes herself throw up."

And with that revelation, I began to make my way back toward my faith. I was desperate for peace but equally scared, because I had stepped away from God, and now I knew what came next. He was going to get me. And he was going to get me good.

We supergirls tend to fear the greatness of God. We don't know how to wrap our minds around his justice. His perfection feels hard and unmoving. We know how messed up we are, and we are sure some retribution is coming down the line for us. We know this is how life works. We screw up? We pay for it. We mess up? We get to clean it up. We sin big? We get punished big. You know how it goes. For every action there is an equal and opposite reaction. Or in my teenage view of God, for every wrong action there is an even greater smackdown coming, since you knew better in the first place and what on earth were you thinking anyway?

This is due in great part to some very scary Sunday school lessons about God's judgment and in even greater part to the Liar. The Liar is so very anxious to keep us in the dark about who God is. He wants to layer our hearts with the belief that God is unforgiving and harsh and vengeful, so he brings to mind all the punishments that we deserve.

"You will most definitely be drop-kicked by God next Thursday for all the gossiping you did with Betty Sue. For shame."

"You are totally in for it. You can't treat your husband like that. You will probably lose a limb in the next forty-eight hours, because come on—anyone who is that mean deserves to lose a limb."

And the thing is that the Liar is right—almost. Each sin does bring a penalty. A price must be paid for bad choices.

At some point we must take responsibility for our poorly thought out actions. But he forgot to mention one thing: Jesus. The Liar really hates when we bring up Jesus. If he could get rid of Jesus, he would. Jesus really makes him crazy. Because you know the lie that we are convinced of, that lie that God is out to get us? It's true. It's just that the Liar left out the good part.

God is out to track us down because he loves us so much he can't let us get away with all our crazy sinning. We are running scared, and he is bearing down hard on our heels in the person of his Son, Jesus. We are sprinting away, full of fear and angst and the knowledge of our wrongdoing, and Jesus is running after us, fast and furious, arms flung open, full of love and peace and righteousness. We fear God's justice, and he is chasing us down with his love. It is what he died for, for goodness' sake. Even in the Old Testament, God used his justice, his discipline, his consequences for one thing: to bring people back to right relationship with himself. Why wouldn't he be after us? He longs to be a part of our lives. Of course he is going to come looking for us.

In John 10:14–16 Jesus likened himself to a good shepherd:

> I am the good shepherd; I know my own sheep, and they know me, just as my Father knows me and I know the Father. So I sacrifice my life for the sheep. I have other sheep, too, that are not in this sheepfold. I must bring them also. They will listen to my voice, and there will be one flock with one shepherd.

Jesus was not satisfied with the sheep that were in his fold. He knew other sheep were out there and the only way they would come home was if he went out and got them. That's because sometimes the sheep ran amuck, and quite frequently the sheep found it difficult to make out the voice of the shepherd. Yes, they did. And for some reason—maybe it was a bad sense of direction or just sheer stubbornness on their part—these sheep had difficulty finding their way back to safety, back to the Good Shepherd and his love. So he was going to go chase them down. With his mercy. With his forgiveness. With his unending grace.

After a stint in therapy dealing with my bulimic tendencies, I found myself on the island of Hawaii in the midst of a discipleship training school at Youth With A Mission. I was sitting on the lanai with one of the leaders as an ocean breeze cooled the night. She said, "Why are you here?"

I said, "You know, I've done a lot of wrong things. I really messed up. I know that God has brought me here to break me. I know there are things in me that need to change."

And my leader began to laugh.

This kind of irritated me, to say the least. Here I had told her I was coming of my own accord, waiting for the hand of God to take me out, and she was giggling.

Then she grabbed my shoulders, pulled me into a hug, and said right in my ear, so that it would be as close to my brain as possible, "Susanna, God didn't bring you here to break you. He brought you here to heal you. He wants to show you how much he loves you. *He loves you!*"

I began to weep. I pretty much wept the entire three months I was there. For three months I waited to be judged, and for three months wave after wave of love was sent my way. And with each message of forgiveness or peace or grace that was spoken to me, I cried. I cried for the truth that was whispered and then shouted in my ear, the truth that completed the half-truth I had been believing all along. God is out to get me, it's true! But he is out to get me because he loves me. He can't wait to chase me down to accept me and heal me and build me up.

The same is true for us supergirls. Jesus is not here to break us down. He knows we are already broken. He wants to lift us up. With his grace. With his joy. With his truth. That truth is that he sacrificed everything—his place in heaven, his life, his will—so that we could live free. The truth is that he lays down his life for his sheep. He is the Good Shepherd. And did you notice that Jesus said he wants to bring the sheep back so that they can hear his voice? This is the beginning of the tired supergirl's journey toward clarity: hearing the voice of the Shepherd. The Liar hates this, because the voice of truth will silence the voice of the Liar. And that is good stuff, people; it really is.

Truth #1: God is out to get me because he loves me.

LIE #2

GOD IS DISAPPOINTED IN ME

J ust this last week I have had a major struggle to overcome. It's a struggle of discipline in my life. Something that lures me away from family and friends has me caught up in the clutches of its tawdry grasp: online solitaire. Even just typing that out, I want to go start a new game right now. I have virtually no self-control when it comes to this game. I know that seems ridiculous. How could a virtual stack of cards have such a hold on me? Honestly, I don't know. When I do actually complete the game and the cybercards go bouncing joyfully across the screen, I enjoy it. But other than that, I think it is just a new way to escape the things I know I should actually be doing, like bills and laundry and tending my children. And when I look at it that way, I feel a bit let down by myself. Disappointed.

How can I veer off course so easily? How can I be lured from the right and good things that lie before me and get caught up in the momentous question of "which black jack should I move over to the queen of hearts?" My own lack of discipline is disheartening. Now, don't get me wrong. I don't think solitaire is evil. Next week it could be bocce ball that has me in its clutches. The part that is so discouraging to me is the realization that I am so easily swayed from the things that matter most to the things that matter least. I am often disappointed in myself, which happens frequently to those of us who have rather high expectations of themselves. Then I think, "If I am this disappointed in myself, how much more must God be disappointed in me?"

The Liar loves this. Yep, he does, and he really goes to work on this lie, laying it on thick. He wants us to doubt how God feels about us. He dims the lights on what is real. He uses witty quips to taunt us, like: "Wow, it really is surprising how you never measure up. So much potential tucked away inside you, and yet here you are."

Or, "I heard that God is really disappointed in you this time. You never cease to un-amaze him."

Or, "I hope he is pinning his hopes on someone else to carry out his grand plan, because your life is fantastically mediocre."

Thoughts of that nature really do tend to wear us down. We feel bad inside when we think that God is looking at us, head down, and saying, "There she goes again. I thought she was better than that."

Tired supergirls everywhere are haunted by the thought that not only do we disappoint ourselves, but we also disappoint our Creator on a regular basis. Almost daily. In cases of playing exorbitant amounts of cyber-solitaire? We disappoint him about every 2.7 hours. We have so many opportunities to make the most of, so many chances to take, and so many goals to achieve in this life. Our track record is less than perfect. Knowing ourselves the way we do, we feel like letting down the Most High God is inevitable. We are so far from the person that he designed us to be, doing the things he would rather we not do, to think that God really is disappointed in us almost seems like no lie at all. We are, after all, tired supergirls. We get tired emotionally, physically, mentally, and spiritually. We fail. We succeed, and then we fail again.

Maybe what the Liar is so keen on keeping us from realizing is what God *is* disappointed in. Maybe it is not so much our lives that disappoint him as the fact that we don't believe he can make a difference in them. Maybe God is not so disappointed in the fact that we fail as in the fact that we don't believe he can actually change us. Maybe he is not so disappointed that we struggle but more disappointed that we don't have faith that he can be our strength in our times of weakness.

When Jesus was living with the disciples, they ate together, walked together, and worked together. Their lives were inter-twined. His life was rubbing off on these twelve men. Matthew 8 gives us a peek into a day in the life of the disciples. Jesus was gathering large crowds who were listening to his teaching, and he healed people. He healed a man with lep-rosy, then traveled on to Capernaum, where he met a Roman officer whose servant was paralyzed. He healed the servant without even visiting the officer's house. Then Jesus and the disciples arrived at Peter's house. Peter's mother-in-law was sick with a high fever, and Jesus healed her too. He went on that same evening to cast out demons and heal all the sick who were brought to him.

The crowd around him continued to grow, and Jesus in-structed his disciples to take him across the lake.

> Then Jesus got into the boat and started across the lake with his disciples. Suddenly, a fierce storm struck the lake, with waves breaking into the boat. But Jesus was sleeping. The disciples went and woke him up, shouting, "Lord, save us! We're going to drown!"
>
> Jesus responded, "Why are you afraid? You have so little faith!" Then he got up and rebuked the wind and waves, and suddenly there was a great calm. The disciples were amazed. "Who is this?" they asked. "Even the winds and waves obey him!"
>
> Matthew 8:23–27

Now, I always thought this was so bizarre and a little bit harsh on Jesus's part when I read it before. Of course the disciples were scared. They thought they were going to die. Who wouldn't be terrified? How could Jesus berate them for that? But then I looked back over their last day together. Multiple healings. Demons gone. A Roman servant healed with a mere word from miles away. A mom so sick with fever she couldn't get up, and at his touch she is up out of bed preparing a meal. This was followed by an entire evening filled with healing, restoring people, and casting out more demons. No wonder Jesus was irritated. Here he had shown them over and over again in one day that he was trustworthy. He was miraculous. He was the embodiment of goodness and rightness and God's supernatural power. He had just lived out the truth "Nothing is impossible with God." And the moment he laid down to take a nap, this all went out the window for them. The disciples reverted back to thinking they were on their own in overwhelming circumstances. They thought that Jesus had checked out.

But here's the thing: Jesus never checked out. He was always aware of what was going on. What riled him up was that after this whole long miraculous day, the disciples forgot to believe in him. They forgot to have faith. Jesus's disappointment came not from the fact that the disciples were imperfect or struggling but from the fact that they doubted him.

We supergirls are disappointed in ourselves. We focus on ourselves, on our lack and our weakness and our inability to perform at the level we think God requires of us. But God says to us, "You are missing the point. Haven't you been hanging out with me, and haven't you seen all the amazing things I have done? What you lack, I have in abundance. When you are weak, I am strong. When you can't perform, I can. I am in control. Always. Even when you think I am lying down on the job. Believe in me. Have faith in me. Put your trust in me. I won't fail you."

The Liar wants to keep us focused on our problems and our shortcomings. He whispers things like: "God has deserted you."

Or, "Clearly, God is so sick of your problems and struggles, he has checked out. You are really in for it."

Or, "God may have helped you in the past, but this is one storm you are going to have to handle on your own. Good luck with that."

The Liar wants us to forget all the miracles God has done in our lives up to this point and think, "I'm in the middle of a storm. God is sleeping. I'm going down."

If the Liar can get us to lose heart, to forsake what we know to be true, to discredit what we've seen with our own eyes, he wins. He keeps us in the dark, plain and simple. If this life is a fight for truth, the moment we falter in believing in the Truth, we begin to lose.

The point when we take hold of God with both hands, owning our belief that in the darkest of circumstances he has us in his very palm, is when we cease to disappoint him. The hard places of life, the daily struggles we face (addictive solitaire vs. living a productive life), the lonely spaces (the thought that God is asleep), the doubting moments (does God love me enough to take care of me?)—these are the times and places we need to start shouting truth back at the Liar.

Ephesians 6:16 says, "Hold up the shield of faith to stop the fiery arrows of the devil." It is time for us tired supergirls to begin sifting the half-truths of the Liar through the shield of our faith. It's time we start shouting some truth back at him.

Fiery arrow #1: "You are a mess."

Tired supergirl response: "Tell me something I don't know. Lucky for me, God loves me and won't leave me the way he found me. I have faith in him."

Fiery arrow #2: "You will never make it. God is asleep."

Tired supergirl response: "Even though I have no idea what he is doing, I have it on good authority (all other 567 times he's come through for me) that he won't let me down. I trust him."

Fiery arrow #3: "You will always be a disappointment."

Tired supergirl response: "So you've noticed my struggles? They are a bit awkward, aren't they? Fortunately, Acts 16:31 says, 'Believe in the Lord Jesus and you will be saved.' It doesn't mention anything about having to be perfect. And I believe that is true."

When we choose to believe the truth and stake our lives on it, we tired supergirls cease to disappoint the One we want to please most—and ourselves too. Our belief in Jesus and his truth frees him up to start doing some miracles in our lives, like loosening the grasp of online card games and helping us love people better. And that is something worth fighting for.

Truth #2: God wants me to believe in him.

LIE **#3**

I CAN'T BE REAL
WITH GOD

A while back, my friend Kara sent me a shirt in the mail. It's a kelly green T-shirt with a giant yellow Big Bird on it. Over Big Bird's head are the words "Keepin' It Real." You can tell by the look on Big Bird's face that he is all about keepin' it real. Big Bird knows how to keep it real. Big Bird doesn't lie. It's not in his nature. I, on the other hand, have some issues with keepin' it real. Sometimes I like to keep it fake. Superficiality is highly underrated. Everyone enjoys life more when it is fake. People ask you, "How are you?" You may have actually had an amazingly terrible day, maybe even a terrible year. However, you know that no one really has the stomach to hear about all the terrible things in your life, and you don't really have the emotional energy to actually say all the terrible things that have gone down in the last year, so you just smile and say, "Oh, I'm fine. How are you?" You know, keepin' it fake.

Four years ago we moved back to the San Francisco Bay area from the greater Washington, DC, metro area. We went from being on staff with good friends at National Community Church, a theater church of eight hundred and growing, to church planting in a high school liberal arts theater that seated nine hundred. Our first Sunday we had forty-eight people. After all of our friends and well-wishers and the onlookers went home, we were left with our original core team. If you counted the core team plus all of our children, we took up eleven of those nine hundred seats. Yep, eleven. We dream big, people.

People would ask us how it was going. We would say, "Really good." We knew planting a church in our area would be difficult. The week we arrived in California, Scott met with three pastors from our area whose church plants had just failed, but still we are hopeful. We tried hard not to judge our success by the numbers on Sunday. But if people were walking their dogs on the high school campus on any given Sunday morning, we thought about including them in our attendance records. They had, after all, glanced our way while church was going on. I remember instances of visitors being driven away by the sheer lack of numbers as they viewed the empty theater. One visitor left with a headache due to an unwelcome whack on the head with a Frisbee. Don't ask. Nothing is as disheartening to a church planter as having no one show up on Sunday except the worship team. It kills hope, tired supergirls; it really does.

We hand-delivered fliers and passed out invitation cards. We prayed heavy, as my mother-in-law, Sandy, would say. But our church growth method could be described as a trickle. If not for the faithful and fearless core team (shout-outs to Glen, Paula, Aaron, Jen, and Dave), all would have been lost. At one point we moved our services back into our house for a year since we could no longer afford the theater payments. While we were trying to be positive about these changes, inside I was full of questions and silent angry thoughts. We seemed to be going backward. I knew Scott was wondering about our next step, but he seemed to take it in stride.

I began to smolder a bit inside. I knew I couldn't talk to God about my issues, for goodness' sake; he was the one who called us to this crazy mess in the first place. I'm sure the last thing he wanted to hear was me whining about how things weren't going exactly the way I thought they should. And maybe it was all my fault in the first place. Maybe if I was a better wife, a better Christ follower, the church would begin to grow more. Church plants were exploding with growth all across the country, so obviously God wasn't interested in hearing from me about my church planting concerns . . . my doubts . . . my dreams . . . my disappointments.

We tired supergirls are used to being fake when it comes to talking to God. We don't want to overwhelm him with our lack of understanding, our nervousness about our situation, or just our sheer inability to grasp how we got into our situation in the first place. We believe we are following the path God has laid before us, so we try to keep a brave face. We try to be polite with our prayers, because we know that he is awesome and really, it would be in our best interest to not offend him. We use soft words and say things like "if it is your will," and "if you wouldn't mind," and "not to be any trouble, Lord, but there's this problem." We're really good at saying the things we think God wants to hear. But then when life gets messy, we're not really sure where to go with it. We don't know where to take our anger, our hurt, or our unresolved feelings when they have to do with him.

The Liar loves it when we get fake with God. He hopes that better yet, we will stop talking to God altogether. I can just see him rubbing his hands together with glee as he starts to darken our hearts with this lie: "Keep what you feel to yourself. Don't let him know you're upset. Then he'll really turn on you!"

Or, "You'd better not let him know that you are angry. He won't like that one bit. He'll probably just leave you in your miserable state and go hang out with a supergirl who has something good to say about him."

The Liar is not ready for us to be real with God. He wants to limit our intimacy, our realness with God. He knows that relationship resides in honesty and trust. If we can't be honest with God, we don't have a chance at a real relationship with him. Contrary to popular belief, God is used to having people who love him let loose with how they feel. He is not offended. In fact, one of his favorite people ever said crazy things to him all the time. God even allowed those things to be recorded in Scripture. If you take a moment to read the psalms, you will be struck by just how real David was with God. He was joyful. He was triumphant. He was mad. He was anguished. He felt misunderstood and deserted by God. And David told God all about it. *All* about it. When we read the words that David penned, we see he was all over the map.

Sometimes David was steadfast in believing that God was in control:

My heart is confident in you, O God; no wonder I can sing your praises with all my heart!

Psalm 108:1

Then there were times that he had peace. He knew God was on his side:

I wait quietly before God, for my victory comes from him.

Psalm 62:1

A few psalms later David was not so sure God even heard him in the first place:

I cry out to God; yes, I shout. Oh, that God would listen to me!

Psalm 77:1

He even got crazy and called God out:

> I eat ashes for food. My tears run down into my drink because of your anger and wrath. For you have picked me up and thrown me out.
>
> Psalm 102:9–10

I'm thinking that if God hadn't picked him up and thrown him out already, he was about to after hearing that prayer. But David knew this one thing that made it all right. The one thing that allowed him to say the things that were on his heart. The one thing that let him open up and say how he really felt. *God loved him.* David wrote an entire psalm about it, Psalm 139. God went before him, remember? He hemmed him in front and back. He knew when David sat down and when he stood up. David couldn't escape from God. If he went to the heavens, God was there. If he was in the depths, God was there. God knew David's every thought.

How is it that we tired supergirls think that we can keep our true selves from the one who loves us most? The one who knit us together inside our moms' bellies? How is it that we think our hurts, our disappointments, our anger, our disenchantment, our boredom, our self-pity, our depression, our rage, our fear, our doubts, our heartaches can escape him? They don't. He reads our hearts. So either we can let him in on the conversation that is going on inside our heads and our hearts, or we can just deny that he is there. But he is there.

David grasped this. He chose to let it all hang out with God. He let everything that was burning inside come pouring out, whether it was praise, thanksgiving, fear, hopelessness, joy, love, or contentment. He poured it out in an offering to the one who loved him best. He kept it honest. He kept it real. And Scripture says he was a man after God's own heart.

40

Even with all the crazy. God was not afraid of the crazy. He was good with it.

Jesus, God's own Son, had a few pointed questions for God in the Garden of Gethsemane. He knew the plan. He'd been in on the plan since the beginning. But the breadth of all that was about to take place had him pinned down with despair. His friends couldn't even stay awake to pray with him. Jesus knew the very heart of God, but he was not afraid to say, "I wish there could be some other way for this to go down" (see Matt. 26:39). You can't get any more real than that. When we allow ourselves to be real, we invite God into our world. We invite real, honest relationship with the one who knows us best.

At around the two-year mark of church planting, when I was riding a hideous wave of postpartum depression, nursing a nine-month-old baby, having Sunday school in my bedroom, and cleaning the house each week so that we could have church in our living room, I began to get real honest with God. I said profound things to him like, "*What . . . is . . . up?*" Because I am brilliant like that.

And, "*Are you kidding me?*"

And I may have even said something to the effect of, "*Get . . . me . . . out . . . of . . . here!*"

At one point I contemplated moving to Hawaii. By myself. I'm sure Scott and the children would have been just fine as I sipped fruity drinks on the white sand beaches.

My new, more fervent prayers sounded more like shrieks and squawks sent heavenward: "Sunday school? In my bedroom? God, you are going to have to help me understand all this." And "How can I go on? I can barely function. I have worn my hair in a ponytail for two hundred and eight consecutive days."

But the craziest thing of all was that he answered these prayers, these crazy cries of a depressed woman's heart. Sunday school is no longer in my bedroom. (Praise the Lord.) Our church continues to grow, at a trickle though it may be. (Hallelujah.) And I have worn my hair down at least five times this year. (The Lord is good.) He has not answered the Hawaii prayer as of yet, but I'm willing to let that one slide.

God heard the cry of the psalmist stuck in a cave. He heard the cry of his Son in a lonely garden. He hears every cry of a tired supergirl's heart, both happy and sad. And he is ready to love us right where we are. Crazy or not crazy. Joyful or depressed. Broken or whole. Fallen or triumphant. We can give the Liar a good, swift kick as far as this lie goes. God is not on the outs with us when we struggle with him. He is on this journey with us, and he is not leaving. He promised he never would. And it doesn't get any more real than that.

Truth #3: God wants me to be real with him.

LIE #4

GOD DOESN'T HAVE GOOD PLANS FOR MY LIFE

In my family, the girls like to plan. My mom, my sisters, Erica and Jenny, my sisters-in-law, Traci and Cheri, and I may not all have the same DNA, but we all have the same heart when it comes to planning. We all get some joy out of planning trips and birthday parties and family get-togethers and scrumptious meals. We find joy in laying out the details and anticipating all the goodness that is about to come forthwith. And more than just the planning, we actually like to share our plans with each other so that we can get excited about each other's plans.

The most recent plan I had been sharing with my mom and sisters was the plan to go see my college roommates, Barbie and Leslie, in Texas for Barbie's birthday. They are also sisters who like to plan. We were going to tour Dallas in all its splendor, starting with the best place to get a manicure and pedicure. Praise the Lord. And then we were going to go out to their Aunt Barb and Uncle Jimmy's lake house and lounge by the pool, taking in nature. Bless his wondrous name. And then we were going to take walks down to the lake and peruse a multi-acre flea market. The largest flea market in the United States. Can I get a hallelujah? The excitement was palpable. This was a fantastic plan. My sisters rejoiced with me.

Then approximately eight hours before I boarded a plane to fly to Dallas, I went to change the laundry from the washing machine to the dryer and stepped on a knife-sharp shard of glass. I always knew the laundry was a tool of Satan. It went into my foot, and the yells that ensued scarred the children and Scott emotionally. Within minutes we were on the way to the ER. And I cried a little bit. Not so much because it hurt. But because this was going to ruin the plan. I knew right away it was the devil's work. Especially when a male nurse with a demonic gleam in his eye scrubbed my cut with an iodine sponge and irrigated it until I yelled out for all to hear, "Sweet Jesus!" and "Lord, have mercy!" I knew the enemy was truly against me when the doctor came in and began to apply the glue to close the cut. I asked him, hopefully and somewhat pathetically (all the while bleeding profusely from my foot), "Do you think I will be able to get a pedicure this week?"

He looked at me a little dumbfounded and said, "Um, no, I don't think that would be a good idea."

I held back a small sob and asked, "What about swimming? Do you think I might be able to go swimming in a few days?"

He then gave me the "Are you straight off your rocker, lady?" look and said, "We are going to need you to keep this dry for the next forty-eight hours and preferably for the next seven days for the glue to do its work."

Oh, the inhumanity! Who would have thought that one small piece of glass could unravel the near-perfect plan of a much-anticipated college roommate reunion? Who would have thought so many of those plans would involve my foot? Who has ever even heard of an iodine sponge? Who was it who said the best laid plans of mice and men—and supergirls—can go completely askew? We supergirls love a good plan. It makes us feel like we have some control and a purpose. We don't really appreciate it when our plans go awry. We have a secret fear that if we don't plan out each inch of our lives that all will be lost. A few of us might even karate chop anyone who messes with our smoothly laid-out plans—God included, because his plan might not line up with ours.

The Liar capitalizes on this. One thing Jesus requires when we ask him to be in our lives is that we give our plans over to him. But the Liar is counting on the fact that our deep love affair with our plans will wither our deep love affair with Jesus. He hopes we love our plans so much that we'd rather keep right on planning and leave Jesus free to impact and change the lives of other supergirls. He likes to hang this lie over the windows of our hearts, cutting off our vision of what God wants to do in our lives. He says, "Have you really thought this through? God doesn't seem to be working in your life right now. Your life is a gong show. You'd better get back to your plan."

Or, "Do you really think God has time to plan things out for you? I think he is just flying by the seat of his pants. I hope the outcome is what you're hoping for."

All these deceptive words the Liar whispers into our thoughts have a ring of truth to them. That's because surely when we look at the days and nights, the ups and downs of our lives, they mostly look messy. And if God is truly at work mapping out our lives, where exactly should we tired supergirls look to find him? Is he working in the daily struggles, or in the deep questioning sections of our lives? Or should we look to find him in the goodness of our lives, the parts where we tend to get it right and the moments in which we soar? Or maybe he could just let us in on the plan, because from where we sit we have no idea where he is going with this.

One of the times I love planning for is Christmas. Christmas usually involves spending time with my family, singing carols, and baking chocolate-covered goods. I love the lights and Christmas trees and 50 percent off sales. I love the moments of giving above and beyond the normal. I love that Christmas is a time of miracles. Angels. A baby born to a virgin. Wise men showing up at just the right time. Unspeakable joy. You know, Christmas. I always think about how God wove so many elements together for one event. But have you noticed that the Christmas story has a whole lot of mess in it?

The whole virgin birth, for instance. Everyone must have thought a bit less of Mary. Such a young girl, getting caught up in sex scandal before she got married. Terrible. Just the fact that Mary and Joseph are so alone in this story is discouraging. Alone with their promise of the Messiah. Alone in their journey. Alone in Bethlehem. And the stable is so gross. The Son of God was born in muck, surrounded by animals. I don't care how cute they paint those cows on Christmas cards, anyone who has visited a dairy farm knows what cows smell like and what the floor of the barn looks like. That sounds like a distinct lack of planning on God's part. You would think that God would have at least had a nice room ready.

But the part that always brings me back around is Mary. Her response to her situation. Her response to God's planning. I'm pretty sure if an angel came to me and told me what he told Mary—that God wanted me to be the mother of his Son, the Son he would use to save the world—I would have said something brilliant like, "You have got to be kidding me! That is *not* at all what I had planned!"

That's probably why God didn't include me in this part of his plan.

Listen to how Mary responds to the angel:

Gabriel appeared to her and said, "Greetings, favored woman! The Lord is with you!"

Confused and disturbed, Mary tried to think what the angel could mean. "Don't be afraid, Mary," the angel told her, "for you have found favor with God! You will conceive and give birth to a son, and you will name him Jesus. He will be very great and will be called the Son of the Most

High. The Lord God will give him the throne of his ancestor David. And he will reign over Israel forever; his Kingdom will never end!"

Mary asked the angel, "But how can this happen? I am a virgin."

The angel replied, "The Holy Spirit will come upon you, and the power of the Most High will overshadow you. So the baby to be born will be holy, and he will be called the Son of God. What's more, your relative Elizabeth has become pregnant in her old age! People used to say she was barren, but she's now in her sixth month. For nothing is impossible with God."

Mary responded, "I am the Lord's servant. May everything you have said about me come true." And then the angel left her.

Luke 1:28–38

We tired supergirls are looking for lives tied up with ribbons and bows and neatly laid out before us. Okay, maybe that is just me. But we do want in on the plan, and we want to have a say. And here is Mary. God is letting her in on the plan. He even sends an angel to tell her the plan. And you know what? She does not comprehend this divine plan in the least. *A baby? The Messiah? Me?* More than likely, her own hopes and dreams had not included the impossible. But instead of asking for say in the plan, or rejecting the plan, or laughing at the plan, she says, "I am the Lord's servant. May everything you have said about me come true" (Luke 1:38).

The Liar is more than a little worried that we will adopt this attitude. He's afraid we will rip his lies off the windows of our hearts and invite God to have a say in our lives. Because if we are willing to accept whatever God has for our lives, then he can actually begin to be able to move in us. To fill us with his Spirit. To change us. He will do impossible things for us and in us because he can. He's God.

I am pretty sure it will be messy. God does not seem to be afraid of a mess. He is perfectly comfortable in a stable or on a lonely road or in a scandalous situation, because he knows it is not the end of the story. God has good plans for us tired supergirls. They may not be easy or neat or fit into our cyber calendar, but they bring life and clarity and love and truth into the world in which we live. And I don't know about you, but I want in on his plan. Even if it's messy.

Truth #4: God's plans for me will rock my world.

LIE **#5**

GOD WILL ASK ME TO DO THINGS I DON'T WANT TO DO

When I was little I had a great fear that God would make me go far away from home to be a missionary. My grandparents were missionaries to India. While my Grandma and Grandpa Foth started a Bible college there, my dad and my aunt, Louanne, attended an English boarding school up in the Nilgiri hills of southern India among the tea plantations. I grew up hearing stories of healing and adventure, of funeral pyres and orphans, of miracles and mystery, of spices and curries so hot they made grown men cry. It was all very wonderful and exciting and, quite frankly, terrifying. I remember one visiting missionary telling us a story about her dogs barking and biting the backs of her calves, and she swung her flashlight around to face a giant cobra swaying from side to side. The dogs saved her life with their barking, but years later she still bore the scars of their frenzied nipping at her legs. This pretty much scared the spit out of me.

I was born in a farming community in Illinois. As far as I was concerned, nothing could be further from my comfort zone than the steamy jungles of India with its tigers and cobras. At the ripe age of seven, I was convinced that all of Asia Minor had a two-to-one spitting-cobra-to-missionary ratio. I thought if I went there, I would catch malaria, since my dad had when he was four. Or maybe I would be trampled by an angry elephant. And all this added up to one thing in my mind: God was going to send me to either Nicaragua,

Malaysia, or Nigeria because that is how God works. He's crazy like that.

Now, the Liar is particularly fond of utilizing this half-truth with tired supergirls. He often likes to paint the corners of our souls with fear. He uses our fears against us. He nudges us and says, "You realize that if you say 'yes' to God and his plan, you can kiss your good times good-bye, right?"

Or, "Did you know that if you follow God, you will become the most boring, overly spiritual person in the universe? None of your friends will come to your birthday party. You will be that boring."

Or, "I'm pretty sure that once God has your ear, he will be asking you to do impossible things like fly to Mongolia. Aren't you afraid of flying? You'd better check into life insurance."

Now, I could just go on and on, because the Liar does so love to go *on*, and *on*, and *on*, and *on*, and *on* about all the mind-numbing, frightening things God will require of us if we choose to follow him. This is one of the most powerful lies the Liar uses to fracture our relationship with God. He knows if he can get us to focus on all the scary things that God will make us do, we will be paralyzed. We supergirls are ready to lay down our lives for Jesus, as long as he is asking us to live the life we choose for ourselves. We'll follow, as long as he doesn't ask us to leave our hometown or take a job that is beyond our abilities. We will absolutely do his will, as long as it doesn't involve public speaking or socially awkward situations. We are perfectly willing to follow God to the ends of the earth, as long as they have a salon specializing in therapeutic massage and a year's supply of *People* magazine there. You know, as long as we can stay comfortable. And with that last thought, the Liar cackles, because he has shut down the good work that God longs to do within us.

Are you ready? Because I am about to drop the truth bomb. This is the truth: God will ask you to do things you don't want to do. In fact, God will ask you to do things you have no idea how to do and that will rock you to your very soul. He will ask you to do things that defy logic. He will ask you to do things that will rip your heart out of your chest and leave you moved and broken and wondering where he will take you next. He will most likely ask you to face your most deep-seated fears. So if that scares the absolute daylights out of you, you might just want to continue on to the next chapter, where we may or may not pursue an easier bit of truth. But if, perchance, you are okay with a little adventuring, read on, dear tired supergirl, because it is about to get good.

When Jesus asks us to follow him, he promises us two things: (1) that we will never be the same and (2) that he will never leave us. When Jesus begins to move in our tired super-hearts, he will ask things of us that we would not normally think of on our own. This is not about him breaking us or asking us to do the absolute last thing in the world we would ever choose (okay, maybe it is), but this is the part where we get to choose. We get to choose if we want to journey with him. Are we with him or not? It is that simple. If we believe the Bible (and we do), we have a choice. We get to choose death or life. Hmmm. Now which do you want? Life is light and growth and truth and change, and quite possibly some discomfort and socially awkward situations. I'm just being honest. And death? Death is staying exactly how we are.

The Bible offers so many examples of God asking people to do things that did not sit well with them. He asked this of Moses, Gideon, and Jonah, to name a few. As they were paralyzed by fear and foreboding, they tried to make wagers with God or back up off the path God had laid out for them . . . but eventually they said yes. Yes to God. Yes to his plan.

Yes to his path. Yes to his vision of what their lives were meant to be. Yes to life. And two things happened: (1) they were changed forever, and (2) God never left them.

Jesus offered his disciples the same choice:

> One day as Jesus was walking along the shore of the Sea of Galilee, he saw Simon and his brother Andrew throwing a net into the water, for they fished for a living. Jesus called out to them, "Come, follow me, and I will show you how to fish for people!" And they left their nets at once and followed him.
>
> Mark 1:16–18

I wonder what went through their heads when they met Jesus. Had they heard about him and his miracles? Were they excited when he approached them? Were they afraid to leave the familiar? Were they scared at the idea of following someone who was nothing like them? Scripture doesn't say. But something about Jesus was so dynamic that they left their livelihoods and followed him right in the middle of the workday. They had no idea what they were signing up for, but they were in. All the way in.

My friend Kristi is an adventurer. She grew up in Africa. She and her husband, Nathan, are raising their boys in—wouldn't you know it—India. We used to meet in the suburbs of Washington, DC, and share afternoon coffee, talking about our little ones, dreaming about what the future would hold. I bet she never thought at that time that she would be riding in a tuk tuk or taking in the Taj Mahal with her boys in tow. But I know that Kristi has realized the same thing the disciples realized long ago: the truth that spending our lives following Jesus is so much better than any other life we could fashion for ourselves.

The Liar is scared to death that we will realize this for ourselves. He's terrified that when God asks us to do something, *we will*. He is hoping beyond hope that we supergirls will keep our lives just the way they are and never step out into that place of freedom and trust that God is calling us to. He is banking on the hope that we won't push past our fears but will stay just where we are. But here is the thing: we can hear Jesus. He is yelling out, strong and loud above the slithery lies, "Come follow me! Come see everything I have for you. You won't believe it. I am going to change you sixty ways from Sunday! Are you ready?"

And we answer, "Yes!" Of course we answer yes. Because really, we can't wait to see where he takes us. I think someday soon I may be sharing afternoon chai with Kristi in India.

Truth #5: God will take me places I could never imagine.

LIE **#6**

GOD CAN'T USE ME

S ome mornings when I wake up, I'm excited about living. I truly look forward to what the day holds for me. I wake from a lovely, uninterrupted slumber and think, "I can do this! I really can! This is a fantastic morning."

And then there are those mornings when I wake up and think, "Sweet hosannas! Where is the coffee?" because surely, I need some caffeine to inspire me. And whoever is making the coffee better make sure to leave some room for cream, because somehow cream in my coffee makes life easier to swallow.

I am not ungrateful for what God has given me; I'm just not sure I have what it takes to blaze a trail of glory through life. Some days life takes me out at the knees. Sometimes the thought of raising young children and teaching them how to tie their shoes seems overwhelming. Other times ministry or finances or health or work or my own expectations about finishing the laundry feel like too much to bear. Some mornings I feel truly uninspired by who I am. Do I really have the goods to get through this life? And how exactly can God use me in the state of imperfection that I am in anyway?

A lot of times I'll take peeks into the days of other supergirls, reading snippets on their blogs or chatting on the phone with friends and hearing how they are spending their lives. I am often amazed at how God has worked in their lives using circumstances, how he has blessed them, and how he has molded them in his image.

One mom at my kids' school, Donna, has ten children. Ten. Children. I feel a bit unworthy to be in her presence because she seems so sane. I seem to have lost a bit of my mind with each child. Clearly, this woman has a tenacity that is to be praised. And then there is Laura, a friend from college, who up and went to Africa and is spending her days mothering orphans. The last time I read her blog, she had just mastered the art of killing a chicken. She is a rock star as far as I'm concerned. Here are these tired supergirls living life on the edge. Sometimes I feel I am living life nowhere near the edge. I'm just mucking it out in the middle.

When I was growing up, I loved reading stories about strong women who let God lead their lives. Catherine Marshall. Elisabeth Elliot. Amy Carmichael. God used these women in amazing ways in spite of hardship and struggle. Reading their stories I would think, *How would I do life as a young widow of the chaplain of the Senate, or as a mom raising her child with the people who had killed her husband, or as a single missionary in India taking in children?* I don't know. I'm sure I would need a bit more than cream in my coffee to walk out a life in the jungles of Ecuador or to be a single mom. Looking at the raw material God has to work with in my life, I'm not sure that God could really use me. I know myself too well. I am overflowing with mediocrity.

This is one of the most beloved lies that the Liar enjoys slathering on. Maybe we already know in our gut that God is out to get us in a good way, but the Liar is pretty good at convincing us that we have nothing to offer God once he catches us. And we are more than ready to believe him.

The Liar slips us lines like, "Do you really think that God could take your raggedy life and make something good out of it? Do you actually think he can use you? That is rich."

Or, "Surely you know that with a past like yours, you have really limited what God can do through you. He may be able to save you, but that's about it."

The Liar is brutal about reminding us who we really are. He loves bringing up all our sinfulness, our lack of smarts, our pitchy singing voice, and our inability to make it through the week without an emotional breakdown. We are so weak in so many ways. Really, how can God use us? And why would he want to? Surely other, more qualified supergirls are out there who could do more for God than we ever could.

I'm sure this is what Peter thought on occasion. Peter denied knowing Jesus three times in his greatest hour of need. Peter abandoned Jesus when he was crucified. You would think that Peter would have just given up trying to do great things for God. But Peter realized something that we supergirls fail to grasp on a fairly regular basis: God can use anyone. God can do anything. God is not afraid to redeem circumstances or people who seem unredeemable. He is not limited by us. In fact, the less we have to offer him, the more he shows he is strong. Peter took this truth to heart and lived it. Somewhere between the time Jesus was raised from the dead and the day of Pentecost when the Holy Spirit filled the disciples, something shifted in Peter's thinking. Instead of thinking, "God can't use me," he was thinking, "I need to be ready when God wants to use me." It shows in this story:

> Peter and John went to the Temple one afternoon to take part in the three o'clock prayer service. As they approached the Temple, a man lame from birth was being carried in. Each day he was put beside the Temple gate, the one called the Beautiful Gate, so he could beg from the people going into the Temple. When he saw Peter and John about to enter, he asked them for some money.

Peter and John looked at him intently, and Peter said, "Look at us!" The lame man looked at them eagerly, expecting some money. But Peter said, "I don't have any silver or gold for you. But I'll give you what I have. In the name of Jesus Christ the Nazarene, get up and walk!"

Then Peter took the lame man by the right hand and helped him up. And as he did, the man's feet and ankles were instantly healed and strengthened. He jumped up, stood on his feet, and began to walk! Then, walking, leaping, and praising God, he went into the Temple with them.

Acts 3:1–8

Now, is it just me, or is this crazy, mind-blowing stuff? Isn't this the same Peter who sank when he tried to walk on water even though Jesus was right there? The same Peter who tried to talk Jesus out of dying on the cross and was rebuked by him? This is the same guy, right? Doesn't he know how many times he messed up, for goodness' sake? Maybe somebody should have reminded him that he had no business being used by God since he was so imperfect.

But this is the brilliant truth that outshines the lie: God is totally used to dealing with human imperfection. He has always worked in and through people who struggle and sin, people who try and then have to try again and then maybe try one more time. He gets it. He is just waiting for us super-girls to say, "This is who I am. You know my stuff. If you can use me, God, I'm yours." And the craziest thing of all is that he will.

Peter was used to coming up a little short in the "getting it right the first time" area. But when the Holy Spirit came upon him and he began to believe that nothing was impossible where God was concerned, one thing was abundantly clear. Peter realized it wasn't about him in the first place. It was about God. Peter knew his limitations, but he had realized that the God he believed in was limitless. He was limitless in his grace. In his mercy. In his generosity. In his goodness. In his power. Peter knew that if he believed in God, really believed, God would honor that and do miracles in spite of Peter's weaknesses.

Peter seemed to stake his life on the truth that nothing is impossible with God. Not speaking in front of thousands. Not recovering from a life of mess-ups. Not healing a beggar by the gate Beautiful. Nothing. And that is the truth that the Liar is trying so very hard to keep from us: nothing is impossible for God, and nothing is impossible with God.

Living a life for God has less to do with being great and more to do with being available. Making an impact in our world has less to do with being talented and more to do with being willing. Changing a life has less to do with having what it takes and more to do with giving what you have to God. The question is not if God can use us but when he will use us. Nothing is impossible with him. And with that truth tucked away in our pocket, tired supergirls, the sky is the limit. It really is.

Truth #6: I need to be ready for God to use me.

LIE **#7**
GOD DOESN'T HEAR ME

The other night I was sitting at the computer, fully enthralled by the magic of email. Will, my middle son, came in, sat next to me, and began to talk to me. While I kept my eyes focused on the computer, I murmured words back to him, like "Uh-uh," "Mmmm," "Okay, honey," and "Sure," until I heard a teary note enter his voice. I looked at his sweet face and realized I had absolutely no idea what he had just been saying to me.

As a parent, I have learned to tune out the whining voices of my children. I am not proud of this fact, but it is the truth. They can put a sound in their voices that can reverberate to the very core of my soul (in a bad way) and harm the eardrums of very small dogs. It can tend to make my eyes glaze over a little bit. But sometimes when I tune out the whining, I also tune out the important stuff. Those would be the words that my children confide in me when they are afraid or feel they have been wronged.

So I turned my entire body to face Will and said, "I'm so sorry, Will. What did you say?"

This prompted a sorrowful tale of Lego structure damage due to his inconsiderate baby brother. I was able to comfort him and right what had been wronged. But I had to apologize to Will. By tuning him out, I had dismissed what was important to him. I had gone into Charlie Brown mode. All I heard was, "Wah, wah, wah, wah, wah, wah, wah."

Because I am human and fallible and don't really understand the mind of God, I am often left to wonder if my prayers have the same effect on him. When I am chatting about my life or crying out for guidance or begging for a miracle, do his eyes glaze over? When I am pouring my very heart out and asking for reassurance, does God go into Charlie Brown mode? Does he hear my desperation, my hope, and my pain, or does he hear an infernal "Wah, wah, wah, wah, wah, wah, wah"?

This is what the Liar has been telling us supergirls for years. He longs for us to believe that God could really care less. He closes the shutters on the truth and tells us that our prayers don't leave the room, let alone pierce the ears of God. And for goodness' sake, God doesn't really have time to hear what we have to say anyway. The Liar whispers in his oily voice, "It's really sad. I'm pretty sure that God *never* hears you when you pray. I mean, he loves you and all. But the way you go on and on? It really is pretty monotonous."

Or, "Do you really think you are worth listening to anyway? Prayer about a pay raise? Wisdom about a relationship decision? Come on! Give God a break!"

Or, "You're repeating yourself again. You just prayed this last Wednesday. God is tired of you. Just be quiet already."

And we believe what he says. Why would anyone, least of all God, bend an ear to our concerns? We might as well take matters into our own hands and fix our own messes. We should just keep our hopes and fears to ourselves rather than bother God with them.

Some of us supergirls think God is a distracted parent who probably just doesn't have time to listen. Or we feel that since he has thirteen bazillion other kids clamoring for his attention, maybe our whining voices get lost in the fray. Some of us simply believe that after all of our praying, he is tired of hearing the same prayers. Because frankly, we are tired of praying the same prayers. We have this secret fear that when Jesus hears us clear our throat and cast up a skittish prayer like "I need some strength over here, Lord. The chocolate is calling out to me," or "Please help us with our finances and help us be the type of parents we need to be," or "God, did you know there is a baby in the hospital hanging on for dear life?" he turns to the Holy Spirit and says, "Oh for goodness' sake, what is she after? Didn't I give her strength last week?"

Or, "Why doesn't she remember that I supply all of her needs?"

Or, "She has no idea what is going on at that hospital. It's covered."

Somehow we supergirls limit our expectations of God and his ability to hear us. We view ourselves as the mosquito in God's ear—we think we bug him.

The very opposite is true. Jesus knew all about prayer. He knew the power in it. He was God in the flesh, he was filled with wisdom and power, and he prayed all the time. And moreover, he knew that his Father was listening. These weren't mindless chants or empty rituals he was practicing. He knew he was in a real, life-changing conversation with the God of the universe.

In the Sermon on the Mount he addressed prayer in two different ways. You can imagine the crowds pressing in, leaning forward to catch his words and hear the inflections in his tone, because here was someone who had caught the ear of God. God listened to this man. They could tell by all the miracles. If only he would teach them the way. Jesus said to the crowd,

> When you pray, don't babble on and on as people of other religions do. They think their prayers are answered merely by repeating their words again and again. Don't be like them,

for your Father knows exactly what you need even before you ask him! Pray like this:

> Our Father in heaven,
> may your name be kept holy.
> May your Kingdom come soon.
> May your will be done on earth,
> as it is in heaven.
> Give us today the food we need,
> and forgive us our sins,
> as we have forgiven those who sin against us.
> And don't let us yield to temptation,
> but rescue us from the evil one.

Matthew 6:7–13

Later he went on to say,

Keep on asking, and you will be given what you ask for. Keep on seeking, and you will find. Keep on knocking, and the door will be opened to you. For everyone who asks, receives. Everyone who seeks, finds. And to everyone who knocks, the door will be opened. You parents—if your children ask for a loaf of bread, do you give them a stone instead? Or if they ask for a fish, do you give them a snake? Of course not! So if you sinful people know how to give good gifts to your children, how much more will your heavenly Father give good gifts to those who ask him.

Matthew 7:7–11

Jesus knew how critical prayer was. He knew how much his life depended on the consistent conversation between him and his Father. It was how he refreshed his spirit after ministering to thousands and healing multitudes. It was the very thing that kept him from temptation when he was in the desert with the Liar. It was what he was doing when he was arrested in the Garden of Gethsemane. It was what kept him focused on the will of the Father. It was an acknowledgment that he was in a partnership, a team of Father and Son. In superhero speak, an inseparable duo. And Jesus could not and would not go forward without checking in and receiving what he needed from his Father.

He invites us to do the same. We need to be a part of an inseparable duo: the tired supergirl and the voice of the Father duo. Need food? Pray. Need forgiveness from your sins? Pray. Need solace in the midst of suffering? Strength during temptation? Pray. You have questions? Keep on asking. It does not annoy God. It really doesn't. The apostle James puts it this way:

> If you need wisdom, ask our generous God, and he will give it to you. He will not rebuke you for asking. But when you ask him, be sure that your faith is in God alone. Do not waver, for a person with divided loyalty is as unsettled as a wave of the sea that is blown and tossed by the wind.
>
> James 1:5–6

So take a quiet moment. Breathe. Empty your heart before the God of the universe. And then—here comes the important part—believe that he will answer. The believing is as important as the asking. And as for the lie that God doesn't hear you, supergirl? Shut the door on that lie. Don't believe it. God is not deaf to you. God listens. He has memorized the sound of your voice. He is doubled over, leaning down, listening for what you have to say. So start talking.

Truth #7: God hears my every word.

LIE **#8**

GOD CAN'T POSSIBLY CARE ABOUT ME

I'm always struck by the largeness of our world. The sheer numbers of the population and the depth of its neediness. Really, if I am being honest, I cannot take it all in. I can't. A hundred years ago people didn't have the same overwhelming abundance of knowledge that we have these days. They were much more concerned about their corner of the map. Automobiles and phones were just coming into their own. Mass communication was limited. I miss those times—even though I was never a part of those times. They sound like good times, except for the lack of running water. That would have put a kink in my need for a good hot shower and a running toilet. But living in a time when people were concerned about their family and friends and maybe a hundred or so other folk who were within walking distance seems manageable to me.

These days, at any given moment I can be aware of a family in crisis in Thailand or the latest hairstyle of the latest star in the latest movie that is the latest hit. I am bombarded with information each time I turn on my computer. And all this information makes me tired. Really tired. All the information out there is not helping me in that area. I was raised to feel responsible for the information that I receive (except for the information about the latest hairstyles; I can let that go). There is so much need in the world. There is so much hurting. Which part do I need to involve myself in? Praying? Fundraising? Child sponsorship? Or should I just turn the channel and ignore it? I'd like to, because my mind is a bit numb from seeing all the needs out there. Thinking about them makes me want to take a nap.

We supergirls are surrounded by needs and joy and sorrow and anger and triumph every day. Each morning we wake to find things have changed in our world. So much life is surging around us, we can barely comprehend it. That leads us to wonder, how can God take it all in? How does he view this mass of humanity that is calling out for mercy and intervention and grace and forgiveness and enough food to get through the day? How can he possibly know at any given moment what is going on with any single person in the world? It seems logically impossible.

Right about now the Liar is getting giddy. He really is. He's getting ready to cultivate a new lie in our hearts. It's the lie that says we should think of God in human terms. He also likes to layer this lie with the one that says we should box God in and try to strip him down to match our own logic. Then he encourages us to doubt God's ability to be more than we can comprehend. After that, he throws his head back and laughs when we begin to question how God can provide for us. He urges us on in this type of thinking: "Other people are far more important than you. You are completely right in thinking that God doesn't have the brainpower to care about what is going on with the AIDS crisis in Africa and think about what is going to happen to you next Thursday afternoon at three o'clock."

Or, "If you really, seriously think that God knows your every thought and thinks of you on a regular basis, you are cuckoo crazy. He picks and chooses who to bless. If he actually is taking a moment to intervene in someone's life or bless their socks off, why on earth would he pick you? He . . . does . . . not . . . care."

"He does not care" is the bitter taste in our mouths we tired supergirls are left with when our own plans go awry or we have been praying day in and day out and things are not changing. The thought "He does not care" shakes our faith when we are feeling surrounded by need and wondering how he can possibly meet us where we need to be met. We despair. Does he care or even know what is going on? And if we are right and he doesn't know what is going on, then why are we following him in the first place? How can he possibly care about the needs of everyone on the entire planet?

Maybe he can care for all of us because he made all of us. Maybe he can care for all of us because he likes all of us. If you read Scripture, you'll see he really does seem to like people a whole lot. Even after they reject him over and over and doubt him and hurt him, he still likes them.

Now, I like people too. I am surrounded by three small people almost all day long. They are getting bigger, but they still tend to cling to my legs or lie on me or breathe very near to my face almost every day. Every once in a while I just yell out, "Everybody give me some room!" This works for about 3.7 seconds, and then I am back to being swarmed. But the thing is, I would do anything for these three little people. I think about them almost all the time. I will do kung fu on anyone who tries to harm them. (I don't even know kung fu, but I'm sure it will come to me if and when I need it.) I am concerned about every part of their lives: their bodies, their minds, their souls. I am pretty much crazy about them. Even when I am tired and cranky and just want to have a moment of peace to take a nap (please . . . just one tiny moment of peace, for the love of Mike!), I am still concerned for them and will often leave my moment of peace and my nap to go make them peanut butter and jelly sandwiches.

Jesus is no different. In fact, he takes this caring thing to a whole new level. He loves us far beyond making us peanut butter and jelly sandwiches. In Luke we find Jesus just re-united with the disciples after they had been out ministering on their own, right on the heels of finding out that John the Baptist has been killed. They were trying to sneak away for a respite. They were looking for a moment of peace in the midst of a crazy schedule:

> But the crowds found out where he was going, and they followed him. He welcomed them and taught them about the Kingdom of God, and he healed those who were sick. Late in the afternoon the twelve disciples came to him and said, "Send the crowds away to the nearby villages and farms, so they can find food and lodging for the night. There is nothing to eat here in this deserted place."
>
> Luke 9:11–12

Now this seems like good, clear logic to me. The disciples were thinking ahead: "Let's send them away. We don't have food here, but they need to eat." Not surprisingly, Jesus saw things differently. He had their need sitting right in front of him. Here they had come all this way, and he was not going to send them away hungry.

> But Jesus said, "You feed them."
>
> "But we have only five loaves of bread and two fish," they answered. "Or are you expecting us to go and buy enough food for this whole crowd?" For there were about 5,000 men there.
>
> Luke 9:12–14

Now, is it just me, or do you detect a hint of sarcasm in the disciples' words, "Or are you expecting us to go and buy enough food for this whole crowd" (verse 13)? The disciples knew their limitations. They were probably thinking, "We're pretty sure we can get enough food together for ourselves, but for five thousand men? That is crazy." Clearly, coming up with that much food was not within the realm of their possibility. Fortunately, these were the kinds of odds that Jesus loved—the impossible ones.

Jesus replied, "Tell them to sit down in groups of about fifty each." So the people all sat down. Jesus took the five loaves and two fish, looked up toward heaven, and blessed them. Then, breaking the loaves into pieces, he kept giving the bread and fish to the disciples so they could distribute it to the people. They all ate as much as they wanted, and afterward, the disciples picked up twelve baskets of leftovers!

Luke 9:14–17

He fed them twice: first their souls, then their bodies. He loved them thoroughly. Jesus cared for their most basic needs and left them satiated. Full. Content.

Unbelievable. I do not have the capacity to take on the hopes, the cares, the dreams of the entire world. But God does. I am not able to provide five thousand people with lunch and have twelve baskets left over. But God is. I do not have the resources to meet the needs of a family in Thailand. But God does. I cannot comprehend the needs of a nation caught in the clutches of a life-ravaging epidemic. But God can. And he will. And he does. And he is. Even now he is meeting tired supergirls right where they are, feeding their souls and caring for their most basic needs. He does not have to bend himself to our logic or be comprehensible. He does not have to work within our realm of possibility. He is God. We may not understand his greatness or his capacity to care for us, but we can believe in it. In fact, we rest in that truth. Our God cares for each and every one of us. He will supply all of our needs according to his riches in glory (see Phil. 4:19). Even our needs for naps and peanut butter and jelly sandwiches.

Truth #8: **God cares about me like crazy.**

LIE #9
GOD CAUSED MY PROBLEMS

One of my favorite things to do is blame other people. I like to blame other people for all my struggles. It makes me feel so much better about myself. If I'm late, I blame my kids. Time management is not my issue; clearly, it is theirs. If they would just learn to put their own clothes on, I would be punctual. And then there is the whole messy house thing—another family issue. It doesn't matter that my shoes can never seem to find their way to the closet. What about everyone else's shoes? If other people would pick up their shoes, then the house would radiate cleanliness. Again, their problem, not mine. And then, as far as struggles with the overeating of chocolate? Genetics. These thighs didn't come out of thin air, people. A lineage of overly healthy thighs harks back to time immemorial in my family line. I'm dealing with a genealogical thigh crisis. You can't just overcome that on a whim. It has nothing to do with the fact that I can down an entire bag of chocolate chips in a twenty-four-hour period. In fact, none of my problems are really my problems at all. I firmly believe that all the things that have gone wrong in my life are because of someone else. Believing this makes it a whole lot easier to be me.

I am not the only one who likes to blame other people. Most of us supergirls would like to blame someone else for our issues rather than just accept responsibility for our actions. It is a legitimate defense mechanism. Global warming? All those other people don't recycle. Speeding? The government made the speed limit too slow. Jeans are too tight? Designers are making their patterns too small and using highly shrinkable denim. Hair won't stay properly coiffed? Defective mousse. Credit card debt? The cost of living is too high. Cheating on a final? The professor didn't give enough study time. Cheating on a boyfriend? He wasn't good enough anyway.

We tired supergirls have a love affair with blaming others for our stuff. We come by it honestly. Blaming was originated by the original tired supergirl, Eve. I love how she just whipped that forbidden fruit off of the tree and got Adam to share it with her, and then when God confronted her with the truth, she blamed a talking snake. I'm not saying I wouldn't have blamed the snake. And I'm pretty sure a chatting snake would have made me want to eat the fruit. I love animals that do tricks. But the blaming didn't stop with Eve; Adam got in on the blaming action by blaming Eve for giving him the fruit. My dad has often pointed out that when blaming Eve didn't get Adam off of the hook, Adam decided to blame God: "The woman *you* gave me made me eat the fruit" (see Gen. 3:12).

When all else fails, blame God. That should go over really well. I think the Liar had probably hightailed it out of the garden by this point (the snake and the Liar are one and the same). But I have a feeling the Liar was thrilled. He was absolutely beside himself with joy that God's new creations were ready to rat each other out. Blame is the Liar's native language. When we start blaming God for our predicament, the Liar really gets excited, because if we are blaming God, we are no longer talking with God. We're just pointing fingers.

Now, most of us supergirls think, "I would never blame God for my junk. I know better than that. I know I got myself into this mess."

But what about the messes we don't get ourselves into? What about all the ridiculous things that happen in life "just because"? Or what about when we are suffering from the poor choices of others? Sometimes we have done every single thing that God has put before us in the best way we know how. We have followed his lead. We've obeyed his commands, and we are loving him with all we've got. And then crazy, terrible things happen, like sickness and failure and broken relationships and death. Maybe we have prayed and prayed and fasted and prayed some more. We have committed his words to heart, we have done all that we know to do, and still we are left in a mess. Foreclosures and divorce and cancer are still our lot. We may begin to think God had a hand in causing our mess when we feel totally alone and betrayed.

Oh, how the Liar rejoices in this, because destruction and despair are his good times. He wants us to think God is the reason for our problems. He slaps this lie on thick and heavy, adding weight to our already heavy hearts. He whispers snaky thoughts into our ears: "God has deserted you after you've always been so obedient. This just doesn't make sense. Look how you have loved him, and he let this happen to you. For shame."

Or, "God did this. You know he is in control of everything. He could have stopped it, but he didn't."

And all we can think is, "This is God's fault."

Supergirls, that is the most lonely place in the world to be. Because if God is against us, then who will be for us? This was exactly what Mary and Martha were thinking when Lazarus died. They loved Jesus. They opened up their home to him, fed him, and gave him a place to stay when he came to Bethany. Moreover, they knew Jesus loved them back. When Lazarus got sick, they knew exactly who to call: Jesus. They knew he could heal Lazarus, so they sent someone for him.

So the two sisters sent a message to Jesus telling him, "Lord, your dear friend is very sick." But when Jesus heard about it he said, "Lazarus's sickness will not end in death. No, it happened for the glory of God so that the Son of God will receive glory from this." So although Jesus loved Martha, Mary, and Lazarus, he stayed where he was for the next two days. Finally, he said to his disciples, "Let's go back to Judea."

But his disciples objected. "Rabbi," they said, "only a few days ago the people in Judea were trying to stone you. Are you going there again?"

Jesus replied, "There are twelve hours of daylight every day. During the day people can walk safely. They can see because they have the light of this world. But at night there is danger of stumbling because they have no light." Then he said, "Our friend Lazarus has fallen asleep, but now I will go and wake him up."

The disciples said, "Lord, if he is sleeping, he will soon get better!" They thought Jesus meant Lazarus was simply sleeping, but Jesus meant Lazarus had died. So he told them plainly, "Lazarus is dead. And for your sakes, I'm glad I wasn't there, for now you will really believe. Come, let's go see him."

John 11:3–15

Throughout this whole exchange, Jesus seemed quite calm. He was not rushed or hurried. He knew exactly how this situation was going to play out. But in Bethany, quite the opposite was true. Mary and Martha were beside themselves. They had called for Jesus to come, and he hadn't. Not only had he not come and healed Lazarus, but Lazarus died and had already been in the tomb for four days by the time Jesus got there. How could they possibly go on? How could Jesus, the one who loved them, allow this to happen? They were completely devastated. When Jesus finally arrived, they didn't even know what to do with themselves. Both Mary and Martha said the exact same thing to Jesus: "Lord, if only you had been here, my brother would not have died!" (John 11:21; see v. 32).

They knew that the source of everything they needed resided in Jesus. Why didn't he show up on time? It was his fault Lazarus was gone. Didn't he care? Why didn't he care? Looking at the story from our perspective, we think, "Just relax, Mary and Martha. Jesus is coming. Everything will be okay. To Jesus, Lazarus is just sleeping. He's going to be raised from the dead."

We tend to stay calm, cool, and collected when we read this because we know the end of the story. Lazarus was miraculously raised from the dead. Mary and Martha got their brother back. It is a totally fantastic story. See how amazing Jesus was? See how great it all turned out even though Lazarus died? They had nothing to fear. God used it all for his glory.

Somehow it feels different when we are living out the craziness ourselves, though. It feels a lot more awful and gut-wrenching when our lives are turned upside down and all that is good and right seems to be missing. We would much rather have God show up when we call or never let these things happen to us in the first place. We feel relieved for the happy ending that Mary and Martha had, but in the midst of living out our own stories, our own crises, our own lives, we can't help crying out, "Where are you, Lord? Don't you care? This is your fault!"

We yell these things at the heavens because we don't have his eternal perspective. We don't understand how everything is going to pan out because we see things so differently than he does. What feels like death to us is merely sleep to Jesus. What feels to us like neglect on his part is his perfect timing for us. God is working out his plan for us supergirls, the ones he loves, in a way only he can work it out. He has not deserted us or abandoned us, or forgotten who we are or where we live, for that matter.

The Liar wants us to think that our lives are spiraling out of control and God is to blame. He wants us to think that God is too late or, even better, that he's not coming at all. But the truth that shatters this lie is that God is in control of our story just as he was in control of Mary's and Martha's. He loves us just as he loved them. He knows what we are going through just as he knew what they were going through. Remember, he is the same yesterday, today, and forever. He hasn't changed. What was truth then is truth now. He will never leave or forsake us. He is not in the dark about what is going on. He knows the end of our story. And don't lose heart, tired supergirls—he is on his way.

Truth #9: God is with me in my problems.

LIE **#10**
GOD DOESN'T KNOW ME

When Scott and I first started hanging out, we would sit for hours talking. And flirting. But mostly talking. I found him to be hilarious. And riveting. Because anyone who can make me laugh? I pretty much want to hear everything they have to say, because laughing is my favorite. Besides, I thought he was cute, so that upped the riveting factor. So we would sit with our homework laid out in front of us, never giving it a moment's glance because we were so enthralled in our late-night discussions about the virtues of Lucky Charms and the reasons why he wouldn't let anyone touch his hair. I wanted to know every single thing about him. Like the fact that he had had a blond afro in grade school—hence the no-hair-touching rule. One doesn't want one's afro to go awry. Or we would talk about how he became a black belt in karate. He even taught me a few moves. (My friend Leslie called it love karate. I denied this.) I wanted to know why he had a deep affection for rap music. All these things interested me. They were all the small bits of history that made up the Scott who was sitting across the table from me.

I also shared some deeply hidden facts about myself with him. Like how in junior high, unbeknownst to my parents, I was the proud owner of a turquoise "I heart Michael Jackson" muscle half-shirt. That I played the flute in fifth grade and still knew how to play the theme song from the movie *Fame*. ("Remember! Remember! Remember! Fame!") And I showed him that I still had the gap I'd had in my front teeth since I was little, even though it was much smaller now. He also had a gap. Obviously fate was involved here.

The more I knew Scott and the more I was known by him, the more secure I became in our friendship. The more time we spent together and the more things we laughed about together, the more connected to him I felt, and even crazier, the more I wanted to tell him things about myself that no one else knew. I trusted him, and I liked him. Whatever he wanted to know about me, I wanted to tell him. Did I mention I thought he was cute?

Now that we have been married over a decade, we know each other's history even more, because we have lived it together. I think there is a distinct possibility that Scott may have a little too much info on me. I don't necessarily want him recalling all my mishaps and bad bang trimmings (case in point: The Bang-tastrophe of 2008) or the fact that yes, I did just have a piece of chocolate cake yesterday, but this minute portion of cake that I am having today is referred to as a smidge, and a smidge doesn't count as another piece of cake, okay? But I feel pretty comfortable saying that Scott probably knows me better than anyone else. We've shared years together. He is in the know, as far as I am concerned.

Sometimes I wonder about my relationship with God. I've spent years with him too—some on the uphill and some on the downhill, some nice and easy and some kind of rough. Or really rough. Still, I can't help wondering if God is aware of all my little idiosyncracies and all the parts that make me who I am. Does he know the reason I twitch whenever I get too near large, flying insects (the 2005 Cicada Incident) or where the scar on my upper lip came from (the Great Rocking Chair Debacle)? Or how I felt on the day I found out I was pregnant for the first time (Best Day Ever Up to That Point)? Is God involved in my life in a general way, where he oversees all the goodness and discipline but then leaves the details for those of us here on earth? Sometimes that is how it feels, especially when I feel he is asking me to do something out of my comfort zone or when I am going through a particularly difficult patch of life. I start to send up reminder prayers, just in case he has forgotten who I am and what I am capable of.

I say to him, "I'm not sure if you forgot this, God, but my tolerance for new situations in a two-month period has already been maxed out. Remember? I'm the one who freaks out with change. That's me. Sue Aughtmon."

Or, "I know you have a lot on your plate, Lord, but the rent is due next Monday. The name is Sue. Do you need my bank account number? I will be happy to give it to you."

Or my favorite, "Not that I am keeping track or anything, Jesus, but my family's already had the stomach flu three times in the last five weeks. Would you mind sending down that hedge of viral protection? This is Susanna Aughtmon, used to be Foth. The one with three kids and the queasy husband."

But what I am really thinking but too scared to say is this: "Do you know me, God? Do you see me? I am right here!"

Sometimes I wonder if he really knows me. Does he know my birthday and the things that make me sneeze? Does he remember that speaking in front of people makes me sweat and that I am a softy when it comes to Hallmark commercials? Does he know what my last four years have looked like and how I got angry yesterday around dinnertime? Sometimes I forget my own kids' names, so I just wonder how he can remember it all.

Usually these thoughts are more prominent when things are not going well in my life. When things are good and life is smooth, when we haven't had an ER visit in a few months and all the bills are paid, I'm pretty sure God has our address.

I feel confident that he is smiling a great smile down upon us and that he is hanging out around our house. But I am human enough to think when life gets difficult that maybe he forgot we moved and still thinks we are living in Washington, DC. That maybe he has forgotten us and left us to fend for ourselves. Or since the good times are over, maybe he wasn't paying that much attention to us in the first place. I know that Scott knows me; I see him every day. But really, does God know me?

I don't even have to tell you that this gives the Liar a whole lot of delight, because he is evil like that. This is a lie he loves to shade our lives with. He does a jig when we think we are a no-name to God. He gets a little happy when we tired supergirls begin to doubt that God is omniscient enough to know everything about everyone everywhere. He likes it when we think God is less than he claims to be. He likes to foster this attitude by telling us, "God doesn't know you. He may have known your mom and dad, but you know what? They served him a whole lot better than you did. I'm pretty sure you are on your own."

Or, "You really should just forget trying to invite him to be a part of your life. You are not that interesting. He has better things to do with his time than keep tabs on you."

This is no different than the way the nation of Israel felt after hundreds of years of waiting for a Messiah and seeing neither hide nor hair of one. They had been told they were God's special people, but through the centuries they had been dominated by nation after nation. As far as they were concerned, God had most likely forgotten them or just didn't care. Their religious practices were tolerated by Rome, the massive city-state that was dominating the scene at the time. Rome led and the rest of the world followed. The Israelites chafed under the knowledge that at one time in their history, they had been the most feared nation. They were the nation led by God—the God who parted seas and cast pharaohs aside, the God who conquered and blessed. But now he had forgotten them, or so it seemed.

But some faithful folks were still seeking God. Some still believed a sovereign God wanted a place in their life, despite the fact that the life they were living out day by day under Roman rule was difficult. Deep in their hearts they longed to hear the voice of God again. They wanted to be led by and known by God. They wanted to be remembered by him. Some had started following John the Baptist. His message felt like truth to them. But he had said himself that he wasn't the Messiah. John said he was only preparing the way for the Messiah. So they kept wondering, Who is the Messiah? Who will be the Savior who knows us and delivers us? Then one day John called Jesus out as he walked by: "There he is. He's the one. THE ONE." John said Jesus was the Son of God. You could feel the excitement begin to build. Could this be it? Could this be the one God promised? Was this the hope they had been longing for? The story goes like this:

> As Jesus walked by, John looked at him and declared, "Look! There is the Lamb of God!" When John's two disciples heard this, they followed Jesus.
>
> Jesus looked around and saw them following. "What do you want?" he asked them.
>
> They replied, "Rabbi" (which means "Teacher"), "where are you staying?"
>
> "Come and see," he said. It was about four o'clock in the afternoon when they went with him to the place where he was staying, and they remained with him the rest of the day.
>
> Andrew, Simon Peter's brother, was one of these men who heard what John said and then followed Jesus. Andrew went

to find his brother, Simon, and told him, "We have found the Messiah" (which means "Christ").

Then Andrew brought Simon to meet Jesus. Looking intently at Simon, Jesus said, "Your name is Simon, son of John—but you will be called Cephas" (which means "Peter").

John 1:36–42

Can you imagine? Your brother has just told you that he thinks they have found the Christ, the one who is the Son of the most high God. The Savior. The Messiah. The one who is going to save Israel from Rome and every other bad thing that has come its way. So you show up to meet him. Breathless. Expectant. This man looks intently at you—a fisherman, a blue-collar worker. And then he tells you your name: Simon. He knows your name. How does he know your name? Did someone tell him your name? If he is really the Messiah, why would he even care what your name is? And why would he care enough to tell you that you will not be the same person you have always been, that now you will be called Peter or the rock? At this point, Peter is in. How can he not be? And then the story gets even better:

The next day Jesus decided to go to Galilee. He found Philip and said to him, "Come, follow me." Philip was from Bethsaida, Andrew and Peter's hometown.

Philip went to look for Nathanael and told him, "We have found the very person Moses and the prophets wrote about! His name is Jesus, the son of Joseph from Nazareth."

"Nazareth!" exclaimed Nathanael. "Can anything good come from Nazareth?"

"Come and see for yourself," Philip replied.

As they approached, Jesus said, "Now here is a genuine son of Israel—a man of complete integrity."

"How do you know about me?" Nathanael asked.

Jesus replied, "I could see you under the fig tree before Philip found you."

Then Nathanael exclaimed, "Rabbi, you are the Son of God—the King of Israel!"

Jesus asked him, "Do you believe this just because I told you I had seen you under the fig tree? You will see greater things than this."

John 1:43–50

Jesus pretty much blew Nathanael's mind. First of all, when Philip came to find him and tell Nathanael that they had found the Messiah, he was doubtful. The Messiah was from Nazareth? That little podunk town? Please. Maybe he went along to see what all the fuss was about. Instead he had his world turned inside out. Jesus called him out. Not only did Jesus speak truth about Nathanael, that he was a man with a heart for God, but he casually mentioned the fig tree where Nathanael was hanging out before Philip found him. You know, the one with the broken branch and all the nice, ripe figs. And Nathanael was awestruck. How could Jesus possibly know this? Obviously this was the guy. The Son of God. This was who they had been waiting for. I'm wondering if Jesus had a little twinkle in his eye when he told Nathanael, "That impressed you, huh? You ain't seen nothin' yet!"

Now, I can understand Nathanael's astonishment. You must remember that there were no background checks back then. There was no OnStar or Magellan or whatever global positioning system device you use these days to find a specific location or person. Unless, of course, you count God. The God who designed the universe. The God who knows who each and every one of us are and knows where to find us at any point in the day. The God who calls us tired supergirls by name the first time he meets us. The God who changes our identity with a single word. The God who speaks truth about us and to us. That God. Then, of course, they had him. He was standing right in front of them in the person of Jesus Christ.

It was enough for Peter that Jesus knew him by name. It made a believer out of him. It was enough for Nathanael to know that Jesus knew his whereabouts and the state of his heart. From that point on he would stake his very life on the fact that good things came out of Nazareth. And it is no different for us tired supergirls. Jesus cares about our lives. He knows who we are. He knows where we live. He knows the state of our hearts. Period. He is the immeasurable God who finds his pleasure in relating to the ones he created, the ones he formed and filled with life. He knows the ins and outs of our days and the work we do and number of children we have. He knows our address, whether it is in Redwood City, California, or Niagara Falls, New York, or Lima, Peru. He knows the very tree we are standing under, and he is looking for us to join our hearts with his. He wants us to stake our lives on the one good thing that came out of Nazareth. And I think we should do it.

Truth #10: **God knows everything about me.**

LIE **#11**
GOD OWES ME

The other morning my friend Bonnie and I were chatting over oatmeal. We were talking about kids and school and ministry and hot chocolate. The important things in life. We talked about working out and parenting books and business. Then the topic of entitlement came up, and we talked about how we are amazed that our kids feel like they should have things. Living in a wealthy area, even though you may not be wealthy, can lead one's children to believe they deserve gaming systems and expensive toys and giant birthday parties. Whatever happened to pin the tail on the donkey? That is my question. This led us to talk about mission trips and inner city outreaches, since we think it's good to expose our kids to places where kids don't have gaming systems and expensive toys and giant birthday parties. Brushing shoulders with poverty can tend to put things in perspective and make you thankful for running water and nice beds and not really care about gaming systems. But then Bonnie said something that really resonated with me. She said, "You know, I don't know why, but I've always felt like I was entitled to having a good life. And I know that is not true. I know that I am not entitled to anything with God, but that's how I have always felt."

That made me take a very deep breath. You know how sometimes when you are talking to other tired supergirls and they are sharing their hearts and their stories, you get convicted? You know, it's that feeling that the Holy Spirit is tapping you on the shoulder and saying, "You should be listening to this. I would like you to take a look at this area in your own life. This is for you. Maybe you should write this down . . . right now . . . with a pen."

I think our Western culture helps us feel entitled to a lot of things. The U.S. Declaration of Independence says we have rights and freedoms. Just because we live where we live, we should be able to have life, liberty, and the pursuit of happiness. And frankly, I like all of those things, and I prefer living in a place that offers me rights and freedoms and life and liberty and the pursuit of happiness. I have visited other countries where they don't feel entitled to any of those things. They may *want* to have rights and freedoms, but that has not been their experience. I have been duly offended in these places when I discovered that they don't care that I think I should have rights and freedoms and life and liberty and the pursuit of happiness. In fact, they have gone out of their way to make sure I know that life in their country is not about my terms and I can take my pursuit of happiness back to where I came from.

Somehow this feeling of entitlement, of deserving rights and a say about what is due to me, has seeped into how I relate to God. After all, I have given my life to him. I write about him. I'm telling my children about him. I try my best to spend time with him. I go to church. I'm married to a pastor, for goodness' sake. Look at all these things I do! Shouldn't God want to give me a good life? Why wouldn't he bless me and keep my kids safe and help me stay sin free? Here I am dedicating my everything to him. Doesn't he owe me?

Now, even typing that out I am a little afraid that a lightning bolt is going to crack the sky and come smoke me right in front of my computer. Because really, who am I to say that the God of all creation owes me anything? But this attitude has wormed its way into my soul.

We supergirls would really like for God to keep up his end of the bargain. Not that he made a bargain, but we kind of have a bargain with him in our heads: if we follow him and give him our lives, then he will forgive us of our sins and give us eternal life . . . along with a nice house and a cute husband, obedient children, and a high-paying job. Or maybe you are banking on some good grades, a nice wardrobe, and an all-expense-paid backpacking trip through Europe. Deal? Now, we are willing to give a little here or there, like maybe the job doesn't have to pay that well, but after all, we are following him. Doesn't he owe us something? (More lightning could be on its way.)

Back in the day, the Liar also thought that God owed him. He kind of wanted to run heaven a little bit. He just thought he was as important as God, that's all. Let me tell you how this went down with God: it didn't. In fact, the Liar and his cronies got the boot from heaven.

In reality, we owe God everything and he owes us nothing. It is because of him that we exist, isn't it? Everything else after that is icing on the proverbial cake. But the Liar would like us to think the way he does. He has pulled the "we deserve stuff" blinds down over our eyes. He would like us to think that we are entitled to a glorious existence because it is our right. So he encourages us on in this thinking, saying things like: "You have taught Sunday school for seven years. You deserve a medal of valor and at least a twenty-dollar gift card to Starbucks. You are totally underappreciated. God owes you."

Or, "After all you have given up for God—the time you've spent serving him, the money you've given to the church, not to mention extra for missions and special speakers, even the way you try to honor him in your everyday life—shouldn't he answer those prayers you have been praying? He owes you."

Or, "You know, God needs to ante up. Here you are giving your all, and what do you have to show for it? What is all that talk about abundant living and peace and heavenly rewards? It doesn't seem like he is sending a whole lot of that your way right now. He owes you. A lot."

Now, this is one of those sneaky lies. It's sneaky because we don't acknowledge its presence in our hearts. If we said this lie out loud, we would realize how ridiculous it sounds. But this is one of the lies that we supergirls live out that seems truthful to us. Shouldn't God give us the best life if we serve him? Or maybe we should rephrase that: shouldn't God give us the life we want to have if we serve him? It seems only fair. But what is fair? Would God give us a life any different than the one he gave his Son?

God has some ideas about what the best life looks like. God values some things that we agree with, like freedom and forgiveness and mercy. Those we will take. But he also values other things that we are definitely at odds with, like sacrifice and turning the other cheek and denying ourselves. If we are modeling ourselves after Christ (and we are), we should realize that the life he chose for himself came at a cost.

> A large crowd was following Jesus. He turned around and said to them, "If you want to be my disciple, you must hate everyone else by comparison—your father and mother, wife and children, brothers and sisters—yes, even your own life. Otherwise, you cannot be my disciple. And if you do not carry your own cross and follow me, you cannot be my disciple."
>
> Luke 14:25–27

Now, that seems a little over the top, doesn't it? Shouldn't there be an ending statement like "and if you do all these things, then everything will always be perfect"? I would sign up for that. But Jesus didn't play around. He wanted people to know that following him, living like him, allowing him free rein in their lives, would come at a cost. Jesus was telling the crowd that if they wanted to be like him, they would have to follow in his footsteps.

"If you want to be my disciple, you must hate everyone else by comparison—your father and mother, wife and children, brothers and sisters" (Luke 14:26).

He left his Father in heaven. He left all that rightfully belonged to him to come to earth.

"Yes, even your own life. Otherwise, you cannot be my disciple" (Luke 14:26).

He loved us more than his own life. He poured himself out for us willingly, without regret and expecting nothing in return. If we want to be like him, we get to do the same.

"And if you do not carry your own cross and follow me, you cannot be my disciple" (Luke 14:27).

Jesus took his life and gave it back to God. He followed God's plans and God's path. Jesus could have done whatever he wanted with his life because he was God's Son. He decided that more than anything else, he wanted us to have the life we were designed for. So he carried a cross on our behalf because he loved God, and he was nailed to that cross because he loved us.

God does not owe us. He has given us his all in the person of his Son, Jesus. And we get to choose our response. It's either all or nothing. Jesus says so. I think we should give him everything, don't you?

Truth #11: I owe God everything.

LIE #12
GOD DOESN'T CARE
IF I AM THANKFUL

My children have mastered the fine art of badgering. In one deep, elongated breath they will say to me something like, "Mom, can I have some chocolate milk? Mom? Chocolate milk? Can I have some milk with chocolate in it, Mom? With some chocolate that I can stir? With a spoon? And not a little spoon. I want a big spoon to stir the chocolate in the milk. A big spoon and some chocolate in my cup that I have right here? Mom, can I have some chocolate milk?"

Deep intake of breath. "Mom?"

And I stand there and blink at them. And then I help them rephrase their massively long and somewhat irritating sentence.

Me: "Mom, can I have some chocolate milk, please?"
Child: "Mom, can I have some chocolate milk?"
Me: "Mom, can I have some chocolate milk, *please*?"
Child: "Mom, can I have some chocolate milk, please?"
Me: "Why, yes, I would love to give you some chocolate milk. Here you go."
Pause.
Me: "Thank you for the chocolate milk, Mom."
Silence.
Me: "Thank you for the chocolate milk, *Mom*."
Child: "Thanks." The child is already on to the next thing.

Gratitude is pretty underwhelming when you must stage the entire conversation for it to take place. I think of all that I do for my kids on a daily basis. I think of the constant care that I provide for them, along with droves of clean underwear and the endless snacks. Don't even get me started on the hugs and kisses, the lavish praise, the tending of Lego punctures, and the myriad of life skills like cutting pancakes and washing hands that I render on a weekly basis. For goodness' sake, where would they be without me? So why in the world is it so difficult for them to remember to say thank you without any prompting on my part? We have rehearsed this gratitude endlessly. I even pepper my own language with loads of "pleases" and "thank yous."

"Jack, will you please clean your room?"

"Will, can you bring your plate to the sink, please?"

"Addison, thank you for putting your clothes in the hamper. Mommy is so proud of you."

See? I am doing what the child development books tell you to do. I am modeling behavior for them. I am acting out the way that I want them to respond to me. Unless, of course, they are paying attention to the way I interact with God instead of the way I am interacting with them. You know, like when I pray and ask God for things. In one deep, elongated breath I will say to God something like, "God, can you please meet our needs financially and protect my family and forgive me and bless my life and clean up all my messes? God? Forgiveness? Blessing? Finances? God, did you hear me when I asked if you would take care of our money? Because I don't know if you noticed, but the ministry isn't particularly lucrative, so if we could just pay our bills that would be good. . . . And then I do have a lot of sins . . . God? Sins seem to plague me and forgiveness would be nice. And if you could straighten out that one thing [insert problem of the week here], you know what I am talking about. You are God, after all, so that really shouldn't be a problem for you. God? Oh, and help me drop five pounds by three o'clock tomorrow. Did you hear me? God? God? Don't forget the blessings, God!"

Deep intake of breath. "God?"

Maybe that is why Jesus laid out the Lord's prayer so neatly for us—because of all the crazy, thankless prayers that were being shot up to heaven. I have a mental picture of him blinking down at me.

God: "God, let your will be done, please?"
Me: "God, let your will be done."
God: "God, let your will be done, *please?*"
Me: "God, let your will be done, please."
God: "Of course, I will let my will be done. I love you so much."
Pause.
God: "Thank you for answering my prayer, God."
Silence.
God: "Thank you for answering my prayer, *God.*"
Me: "Thanks." I am already on to the next thing.

We tired supergirls often get so caught up in the business of life that when our prayers are answered, we are already on to the next thing. The next prayer request. The next plan. The next day. The next week. We rarely take time to pause and thank God for all that he has done for us, not just in answering the prayer but on a regular basis. His care of us. His direction. His protection. His grace that he has poured out on us. His mercy that he renews every morning. The breath that fills our lungs. Our ability to see and speak and hear and run and dance. Well, maybe some of us can't dance. But some of us know how to get our groove on, and we can be thankful for that.

Here is the thing: the list of items that we could be thanking God for each and every day is endless. Really. If you are reading this book, I am pretty sure that you are alive. That in and of itself is something that deserves a great deal of thanks. But most of us tend to whip through life on autopilot, taking everything from breathing to gasoline pumps for granted. That is how blessed we are. We are so blessed we don't even recognize it, or we are so overwhelmed by the answered prayer that we just take it and run with it, forgetting to thank the one who answered the prayer.

The Liar has a heyday with this. He would like us to spend as little of our time as possible thinking about God and his goodness. The fact that God is so gracious really rankles the Liar. So he tries to black out any praise we feel compelled to give. He would like to keep our gratitude on the down low. He spurs us on in our thanklessness, saying, "Don't even bother thanking God. The fact that you weren't hit by that crazily swerving car was a coincidence. You weren't really in danger in the first place."

Or, "It's really not that big of a deal that you are healthy. Most people are healthy. It's because you take such good care of yourself. You just exercised yesterday. God doesn't really have anything to do with it."

Or, "You know God doesn't really hear your prayers in the first place, so how can you really think this has anything to do with it? This is luck. You are lucky. You know what? Why don't you thank your lucky stars? They would appreciate a good thank-you."

But believe it or not, there were no lucky stars on hand when Jesus healed ten lepers. The only provider of grace and healing present in this story was Jesus. He was making his way toward Jerusalem, and he came upon a group of people who needed him. Everywhere he went people needed and wanted things from him. People constantly pleaded with him to bless them and touch their lives in miraculous ways.

> As Jesus continued on toward Jerusalem, he reached the border between Galilee and Samaria. As he entered a village there, ten lepers stood at a distance, crying out, "Jesus, Master, have mercy on us!" He looked at them and said, "Go show yourselves to the priests." And as they went, they were cleansed of their leprosy. One of them, when he saw that he was healed, came back to Jesus, shouting, "Praise God!" He fell to the ground at Jesus' feet, thanking him for what he had done. This man was a Samaritan. Jesus asked, "Didn't I heal ten men? Where are the other nine? Has no one returned to give glory to God except this foreigner?" And Jesus said to the man, "Stand up and go. Your faith has healed you."
>
> Luke 17:11–19

Here are ten men who had been on the outskirts of real living. Due to their leprosy, they were not allowed to come into contact with people who were well. They knew their deficiency. They stood back from Jesus as he came into town, but you can be sure that they made themselves known. Ten men crying out is quite a sound. It had to have been a roar as they yelled out, "Jesus! Over here! Have mercy on us! Look over here! We need your help. Don't forget to help us! Master! Jesus?"

And guess what? He healed them. They would never be the same. They would be radically changed forever. This was good stuff. But the story didn't end with the healing. Jesus was fully aware of what had taken place, and when only one man returned, and a Samaritan at that, Jesus asked, "Didn't I heal ten men? Where are the other nine?" (Luke 17:17). I can almost imagine him calling out after them, "No problem, other nine guys I healed! Don't bother saying thanks, even though I restored your life to you in a hugely miraculous way."

Okay, Jesus probably wasn't as sarcastic as I am. But it should come as no surprise to us that Jesus cared if all ten men said thank you. Of course he cared. We know because we are made in his image and we would care. We care if people thank us or if they ignore our generosity. He is no different. He cares about our response to him. He cares that we recognize he is in our corner. He cares if we grab our answered prayer and run with it or if we take the time to turn and come back to say, "Thank you, God. Praise you! Yippee!"

The way that we show him our recognition of his miraculous hand on our lives is by thanking him. Gratitude. He deserves our thanks, especially after he has granted us new lives and all. Just like I would like a small thank-you from my boys for the act of giving them some milk with a big spoon to stir in the chocolate, God appreciates when we recognize his goodness to us. It cements our relationship. We are in this thing together. He is providing for us tired supergirls, and we get to be truly grateful for all that we receive from such a magnanimous God. He loves providing for us. It would behoove us to show him how truly thankful we are for that provision; for all the breathing and scrumptious food and mercy and forgiveness and eternal life.

So how about it? A prayer of thanks. Right here. Right now. That will really tick the Liar off.

> Creator God,
> Thank you for who you are. Thank you for sending
>   your Son.
> Thank you for giving us grace for each day.
> Thank you for giving us new mercies each morning.
> Thank you for air and health, for transportation and
>   comfortable beds.

Thank you for always coming through, for endurance, for opportunities and work (even though work makes us crazy sometimes, we are still thankful).
Thank you for food for our bellies and good fiction with witty banter.
Thank you for friends who make us laugh and for families that love us no matter what.
Thank you for chocolate. . . . I really mean that. . . .

Once you get started it's hard to stop. We could go on and on. Why don't we?

Truth #12: **God loves when I am thankful.**

LIE **#13**

GOD DOESN'T FEEL THINGS LIKE I DO

I talk on the phone with my cousin Beth a lot. She is one of my favorite supergirls. She has known me from birth, so I can pretty much tell her anything. These days life seems to be so full of cares. It is full of more cares than I can handle on my own. Sometimes when I am feeling a little lost and a lot overwhelmed, I call Beth and say, "I think I am going crazy." And she laughs because she knows that when we lose our minds caring about things, a good laugh can help. That's just how it goes with us. Sometimes when life lays us flat with all of its stuff—like bills and raising small children and fears about what next Tuesday has in store for us—we call each other to talk it out.

When I say "I think I am going crazy," Beth never hangs up on me. Beth has the ability to listen to whatever I am saying and encourage me. I know that no matter what, she is on my side. She always says something uplifting like, "Even if you are totally crazy, I still love you."

I say things to her like, "I would like to move to Hawaii, where I would be very tan and read a lot of fiction and drink tropical beverages by the pool. And when I got tired of the pool, I would go to the beach and get even more tan, and then I would nibble on some chocolate-covered macadamia nuts, and everything in the world would fall magically into place, and I wouldn't have to feel bad things anymore."

When I say this, she doesn't even bat an eye, because sometimes she would like to go to Hawaii herself. I know that Beth understands me and accepts me, and she cries with me when

I cry. When someone is willing to share your pain, you know you have found a friend. I love having Beth on my side.

But in the dark days (and I do have some), when I feel alone in all that I am feeling and I am not talking to Beth about it, I talk to God. I lay out all my crazy to him. I tell him I am pretty sure I have lost most of my mind and the rest is sure to follow. I tell him I didn't handle yesterday very well and I'm not sure how tomorrow will go down.

Now, I know Beth feels the same way that I feel about things because we are made up of the same stuff. We even share some DNA. But I'm not so sure about God. How can a holy, all-knowing, all-powerful God feel what I feel? Sometimes I don't think we have much in common. I don't know anything; he knows everything. I have no control; he has all control. I have no superpowers; he is all-powerful. How can the one who has all the power, love, and knowledge in the world feel sad or lonely or humbled?

In these dark, lonely moments when I am doubting and afraid, I think things like, *How can he relate to a half-crazy mom of three living in a rental on the San Francisco Peninsula? And why do I have to feel things so much? Sometimes feeling things deeply really stinks.*

We tired supergirls feel things all the time. We feel sad. We feel lonely. We feel underappreciated. We feel stressed out. We feel hurt. We feel angry. We feel misunderstood. Sometimes life seems to layer itself so heavily that we can't get out from underneath all these feelings. And I'm not even talking about hormones. Don't even get me started on the hormones. I'm just talking about the wide range of emotions we experience on a daily basis, like how we feel so strongly about our family and friends and their joys and sorrows.

Does God know that anxious feeling we have that wakes us up at night thinking about our boyfriend who is battling depression? Or how about that pain in our stomach we get when we listen to our sobbing child describe being teased endlessly at school? Or the blazing anger that comes after that conversation with our child because we would like to go teach those kids a thing or forty about kindness and acceptance? Or how about the despair we feel when our best friend calls to say her husband has left and she's not sure he's coming back?

And really, how is God impacted by what is going on down here? Does he feel what we supergirls are feeling? Does he understand the pain and the anger we feel when the guy we loved so much walks out? Does he have that wrenching feeling in his gut when our house is foreclosed on? Does he know how lonely we are when all our friends are married and we still haven't met the one? Or is he in Hawaii sipping tropical beverages by the pool? Maybe he is so vast and unfathomable and great that our hurts and longings don't even faze him. Maybe he can just shake it off. Maybe he is not like us at all.

This is the half-truth that the Liar perpetuates on a daily basis. He likes to spray a fine mist of despair in our hearts with the thought that God is not invested in us at all. He encourages these feelings in us, saying things like, "If God felt what you felt, surely he would do something about it. Don't you think?"

Or, "God has all the power in the world—do you think your little heartbreak is going to concern him at all? He protects himself against feeling all your stuff. Otherwise, how could he deal with so much pain in the world?"

Or, "He is not human. Of course he doesn't feel what you feel. He has no idea what you are going through right now."

But that is where the Liar slips up. That is when we supergirls can know that we are dealing with a big fat liar, because in fact, God became human. Paul talks about Jesus like this:

> Though he was God,
> > he did not think of equality with God
> > as something to cling to.
> Instead, he gave up his divine privileges;
> > he took the humble position of a slave
> > and was born as a human being.
> When he appeared in human form,
> > he humbled himself in obedience to God
> > and died a criminal's death on a cross.
>
> Philippians 2:6–8

God is not unfamiliar with the human condition. Jesus does not wonder how we feel when bad things happen to us. He knows what it feels like in the very core of his being because he lived it. He felt cold and lonely and wet and hungry. He felt happy and angry and surprised and hot. Is anything more incredible than realizing that the one who didn't have to feel bad, ever, decided that he would like to anyway because he wanted a relationship with us? Is anything more crazy than realizing that the one who spoke galaxies into being decided he would like to eat some fish on the beach with the people he created? Or that he wanted to experience what it felt like to have rain hit his forehead? Or that maybe he experienced anger welling up in him when he heard people saying catty things about his mom and where she said he came from? Or that he understood the sting of rejection since the people who lived in his town wouldn't believe he was who he said he was? Why would he choose to feel so much? It's unbelievable, really.

The Liar is hoping we will not believe it, because if we realize the truth, the jig is up. He is hoping we will not believe that God lived where we lived, that he feels what we feel, that he understands every single triumph and struggle that we go through. But whether or not we believe it, it's the truth. God was here. He gets it. It is the single truth that our faith hinges on: God became man. And all of these feelings and emotions that course through our bodies on a daily basis also coursed through his body. He had the right to live in heaven and never have to experience any of the brokenness of humanity that came by way of sin. But he made himself nothing so he could know how we feel and so that he could enable us to live the life that is promised to us when we believe in him.

So one more time, we get to give the Liar the boot, because we can believe this: that Jesus came to earth. We can believe that he knows what it feels like to be abused and lied to and tricked and treated shabbily. We can believe that he knows what it feels like to care about his mom and his friends and to be concerned about what life had in store for them. We can believe that he knew what it felt like to hold someone's hand or to touch the downy hair on a baby's head or have laughter welling up in his belly when something struck him funny. We are made in his image. We feel all these things. He feels all these things. We are more like him than we know. The Bible says he is not afraid to feel things on our behalf. And in human form he humbled himself even further by dying a criminal's death on a cross (see Phil. 2:8).

He humbled himself for us. He gave himself for us. He felt more than we can ever imagine. He feels what we are going through right now. And the best part is? He is willing to share our pain. He is our friend. God is on our side.

Truth #13: **God feels what I feel.**

LIE #14
I WILL NEVER
BE ENOUGH

I had one primary focus in junior high. That would be junior high boys. I remember hoping beyond hope that the boy that I liked would like me back. That he would ask me to "go with him," as it were. Even though I was only eleven, I was very aware of the fact that not a lot of love was being sent my way. While my friends "went" with boys, holding hands and writing notes, I got nothing. The most attention I got in sixth grade was a half-hearted couple's skate with a very nice boy who did not like me one iota. God love him, I believe he asked me to skate because he felt sorry for me. And goodness knows I had nothing to offer him in the way of clever conversation. I could barely look at him as we skated around the rink. All I could think about was willing my hand to stop sweating and throwing up desperate prayers of, "Dear God, please don't let me fall!"

In seventh grade, my best friend once asked a boy if he would ask me to "go with him." I can still feel the awkwardness of that exchange in my chest at this very moment. Sweet mercy, that's a terrible junior high memory! He was very kind, bless his heart, but he declined.

In those fateful days of junior high purgatory, I began to look for a way to change myself so that I would be more beautiful or lovable. I felt that surely my life would change if I could only get rid of my glasses and wear a three-tiered miniskirt. I had entered seventh grade with an extremely round pair of glasses and a quilted Jessica McClintock jacket. In the two years between entering seventh grade and graduating eighth grade, I grew six inches, shed my glasses, and inherited a pair of wedge Cherokee sandals from my sister, Jenny. My dad was not down with the miniskirt idea, but I was sure that love was just around the bend anyway because now I had style.

Now people did take note of my contacts. Teenagers really will become your friend if you get better looking. But no new love was forthcoming, so I kept changing things up. There had to be something I could do to get someone to like me. In high school I had a revelation: the solution to all my problems was a spiral perm. You do not want to know how many perms I endured throughout high school. Not one of those perms merited me a boyfriend. In college, weight became the issue: if I could just lose some weight, then I would have a boyfriend. In fact, I graduated from high school and made it through three years of college and a few semi-horrendous pseudo-relationships without ever having a real boyfriend. It didn't matter how tight my perm was or what number showed up on the scale.

By the end of my junior year in college, I came to the conclusion that I was not enough. Not beautiful enough. Not witty enough. Not attractive enough to hold a man's attention. And while I had many God-given gifts and talents and many things to be thankful for, I couldn't get past my own less-than-ness. I couldn't understand why some people had relationship after relationship while I had nothing. I couldn't fathom why something I had longed for had never come to pass for me. I didn't see how being alone could be a positive. I saw my lack of a relationship as a deficit in who I was. This lie worked its way into my very soul and slithered its way into my relationship with God.

Supergirls everywhere believe this lie on a daily basis—that we are not enough. Some supergirls believe they will never be strong enough to meet the needs of their family. To succeed in life. To go after the career they long for. Some believe they will never be beautiful enough, confident enough, or engaging enough. They believe they will never be smart enough to make their mark on the world or competent enough to complete a task they have taken on. They fully believe that no matter how hard they try, no matter how much they improve themselves or change their circumstances, they are not enough. Period.

The Liar is absolutely ecstatic about this. He is almost frantic with happiness. He can barely breathe, he is so excited by this prospect. This could be his best lie yet, because with this lie he has us completely wrapped up in ourselves and our inabilities. Any time he can get us to take our eyes off of God, he high-fives himself. He encourages this line of thinking with whispers like, "It's true. You are not enough. Even when you try really hard, you will never be enough. In fact, I'm not even sure where you came up with the idea that you ever *could* be enough. It's not going to happen. At least not in your lifetime."

Or, "Maybe you should go to that seminar in February and learn everything you possibly can about how to change who you are, because this person you are right now really isn't working for you. You are kind of pathetic."

Or, "You really should spend more time with your friend Susie, because she is enough. Maybe if you hung out with her, it would rub off on you a little bit."

The Liar also likes to remind us about other people we think have it all together or the people we think are enough. He uses other people's successes to remind us of our failures, their abilities to remind us of our inadequacies. He wants us to lose ourselves in our lack and our less-than-ness, and he will use whatever means he can to achieve this.

Now, the apostle Paul didn't buy into this lie. In fact, a flood of truth filled his heart in regards to his less-than areas. He had an even crazier take on his more-than areas. Paul was very aware of all the amazing things in his life that he could boast about, but that was not what he focused on. Paul had a pedigree. He was a Roman citizen. He was a Jew's Jew. He was a servant of Christ. He had been beaten, flogged, imprisoned, shipwrecked, and more, all in the name of Christ. But this was not what he focused on, which is funny to me because if I was that awesome, I think I would want to tell a few people about it. You know, because I was so awesome. It's hard not to brag when you are truly awesome. But instead Paul asks in 2 Corinthians 11:29–30, "Who is weak without me feeling that weakness? Who is led astray, and I do not burn with anger? If I must boast, I would rather boast about the things that show how weak I am."

Clearly, Paul had spent one too many days in solitary confinement. Did he even know what he was saying? Apparently, he did. Paul was a Christian superstar. But instead of bringing attention to his awesomeness, he chose to brag about his areas of weakness, the deficits in his own life, the things that made him stumble. He didn't see them as a deficit. He saw them as an opportunity. He went on to say,

> If I wanted to boast, I would be no fool in doing so, because I would be telling the truth. But I won't do it, because I don't want anyone to give me credit beyond what they can see in my life or hear in my message, even though I have received such wonderful revelations from God. So to keep me from becoming proud, I was given a thorn in my flesh, a messenger from Satan to torment me and keep me from getting proud. Three different times I begged the Lord to take it away. Each time he said, "My grace is all you need. My power works best in weakness." So now I am glad to boast about my weaknesses,

so that the power of Christ can work through me. That's why I take pleasure in my weaknesses, and in the insults, hardships, persecutions, and troubles that I suffer for Christ. For when I am weak, then I am strong.

2 Corinthians 12:6–10

Paul's attitude toward the things that laid him low was about the exact opposite of the regular supergirl's attitude toward weakness. We are supposed to be super, right? We don't want to be less than. We want to be more than. But Paul took the slick words of the Liar and turned them on their ear. He said, "I am not enough. But that is okay. God is." Instead of concerning himself with his inabilities, he saw them as an opportunity to look to God's abilities. He had plenty to be proud of in his life, but he would rather be proud of who God was than who he was. When we yield our inabilities to God, we give him a chance to do his stuff—his great, perfect, wonderful, marvelous stuff.

Even while writing this chapter, I have been struggling. I've been searching for words and phrases and ideas to share. All but two hours ago, I threw up my hands and said, "Good grief! I have no words. I have nothing to say. I'm done."

I have this feeling that God just kind of smiled at that moment and said, "Finally, now I can get to work. Would you like to ask me for some words and phrases and ideas to share? I might have something to say on the matter. In case you haven't realized, my grace is sufficient for you."

I'm pretty sure that another word for sufficient is *enough*. He is enough for us. His grace is not just dealt out when we sin. It is dealt out on a moment-by-moment basis. It is enough to fill all the needs and holes and inabilities that we have. Remember Moses and his stuttering? Grace. Remember Rahab and her reputation? Grace. Remember Peter and his big fat mouth? Grace.

As for me, around about my twenty-third year, I decided that if God had a guy for me, then he could bring him my way when he wanted to. I was done with going after guys who just weren't that into me. I came to the conclusion, after a lot of soul searching and talks with Jesus, that I was okay with who I was. I wasn't perfect, but then neither was anyone else. And I had kind of settled in myself the thought that if someone didn't think I was enough just as I was, he could just move along. I even went so far as to have the thought that if it ended up being just me and God, he would help me be okay with that too. God saw fit to pour out his grace to me in the person of Scott Aughtmon, a man who saw me, imperfections and all, and loved me anyway. Even though I am not enough, God is.

God meets us tired supergirls at our point of insufficiency and pours out his strength. In our relationships. Our self-esteem. Our personalities. Our abilities. Our questions. What is imperfect in us, he can perfect. What is lacking in us, he can fulfill. He loves to show his strength in our weakness. This makes the Liar a little bit cuckoo for Cocoa Puffs, because he hates when we recognize our own less-than-ness as an opportunity for God to show his greatness. Then we get to know, beyond a shadow of a doubt, that his grace is sufficient for us no matter what situation we are in. And there's one more thing: we get to breathe a sigh of relief, because he is enough.

Truth #14: God is enough.

LIE **#15**

I CAN LOVE PEOPLE AT MY CONVENIENCE

S ome days I feel pretty good about myself. I'm kind to my children. I love my husband. I go out of my way to help someone less fortunate than myself. I pray for my friends and family. I put all that I have into caring for the people God has put in my life. I look at myself and think, "Now this is how it should be." And I let out a deep sigh of satisfaction that for this one moment in time, I am not totally letting God down.

But every once in a while, I get a real vision of who I am in regards to loving. Okay, it's not every once in a while; it's every Sunday. Every single Sunday I feel like I am right on the brink of a nervous breakdown. I almost always feel like I've lost my salvation and the ability to care for my fellow humans all in one fell swoop. Sunday mornings kill the love. I don't know if it's because I have to get our three children ready by myself or because I have to be somewhere on time. Or maybe it is the fact that I am trying to prep for a Sunday school lesson and the devil has set his minions to play at my very doorstep. But I'm just going to lay it all out for you: there are moments when if I could opt out of Sunday mornings, I would. Not because I don't like Jesus and his people. I really do. But the bedlam of Sunday mornings often seems to leave me unable to love people the way I should.

Case in point? This last Sunday morning. Scott was already gone. I was putting the finishing touches on the Sunday school lesson. I had the children up and dressed. Will had a complete emotional breakdown over the breakfast cereal that was being offered. Wailing. Gnashing of teeth. It was not pretty. He was dispatched to his room to calm himself down (or so I could calm myself down). It was just cereal. We don't do a three-course breakfast on Sunday morning. It's all about survival. You gotta do what you gotta do and get to church. Then Jack could not find his shoes. He could find one shoe of three different pairs of shoes. It was fifty degrees outside. I told him to wear his flip-flops, because we live in California and I knew it would warm up eventually. Breakfast wound down, teeth were brushed, and we were finally loading up. Addison, who is currently potty training, had a potty training catastrophe. All I'll say about that is that we had to unload and take a bath. Can you feel the love slipping away, tired supergirls? Because it was.

At this point the television came into play because I was not creative enough to think of a way for the other children to occupy themselves while I was giving Addison a bath. Turning off the television then caused another meltdown since it happened mid-show. The younger two children took turns crying all the way to church. We finally arrived, and the boys ran ahead of me and attacked the doughnut table like a herd of voracious wildebeests. I will go so far as to say there may have been some grunting, and the other parents who were standing nearby looked shocked. I was shocked. The love was completely gone at this point.

Then the weeping began. Surprisingly enough, it was not me weeping. Will and Addison wanted the same chocolate doughnut with red sprinkles. Will was unwilling to go halfsies. In my world, if there is one chocolate doughnut and two children, you are going halfsies or you can have some air to eat. Air is always an option if you are not willing to share. The children were working on my last Sunday nerve. I ripped the doughnut in half. Cries of despair rang out across the lobby, and being the cold-hearted, unfeeling Sunday mother that I am, I said something very kind like, "If you don't stop crying right now, you are on time-out for life," or something to that effect. I was angry and embarrassed. Tired and impatient. I had no love. Not even a little droplet of like. I was altogether un-Christlike in my manner toward my children. All I wanted to do was load them back in the car and beat a hasty retreat back to the house.

We tired supergirls have so much on our plates with friends, family, children, work, school, finals, grocery shopping, phone calls, and text messages (some of us are very slow at texting, so if you could just stick to the phone calls, we would appreciate it). How exactly can we be expected to love those people around us who are clamoring for our attention? We are hard pressed on every side. It is all we can do to get ourselves out the door. How can we be expected to love people on top of that?

The Liar has an easy solution for us supergirls: don't. Don't love people when it gets too hard. Do what you need to do and get on with your life. You have places to go and people to see; you have responsibilities and you have deadlines. Who in heaven's name has time for sacrificial love? The Liar's favorite part of this lie is the part that says, "You can love people when it is easy for you." He has us thoroughly convinced that we can love people on our own terms, when it is most convenient for us. He affirms our thoughts with his own: "Do they really need you right now? Really? You have somewhere you need to be. You can get around to listening to that person on your lunch break."

Or, "I know that God said to be loving, but he meant in easy situations. Clearly you have too much going on in your life. You can be loving next time."

Or, "You have given and given and given. And then you have given some more. You have filled your love quota for the day. Tell them to come back tomorrow."

Did I mention that the Sunday school lesson I was teaching was on loving your neighbor as yourself? I feel very distinctly that when Jesus told the story of the Good Samaritan, he was not taking into account crazy, out-of-control Sunday mornings. Or maybe he was talking exactly about Sunday mornings.

One day an expert in religious law stood up to test Jesus by asking him this question: "Teacher, what should I do to receive eternal life?"

Jesus replied, "What does the law of Moses say? How do you read it?"

The man answered, "'You must love the LORD your God with all your heart, all your soul, all your strength, and all your mind.' And, 'Love your neighbor as yourself.'"

"Right!" Jesus told him. "Do this and you will live!"

The man wanted to justify his actions, so he asked Jesus, "And who is my neighbor?"

Jesus replied with a story: "A Jewish man was traveling on a trip from Jerusalem to Jericho, and he was attacked by bandits. They stripped him of his clothes, beat him up, and left him half dead beside the road.

"By chance a priest came along. But when he saw the man lying there, he crossed to the other side of the road and passed him by. A Temple assistant walked over and looked at him lying there, but he also passed by on the other side.

"Then a despised Samaritan came along, and when he saw the man, he felt compassion for him. Going over to him, the Samaritan soothed his wounds with olive oil and wine and bandaged them. Then he put the man on his own donkey and took him to an inn, where he took care of him. The next day he handed the innkeeper two silver coins, telling him, 'Take care of this man. If his bill runs higher than this, I'll pay you the next time I'm here.'

"Now which of these three would you say was a neighbor to the man who was attacked by bandits?" Jesus asked.

The man replied, "The one who showed him mercy."

Then Jesus said, "Yes, now go and do the same."

Luke 10:25–37

Now, first of all, I think it is funny that the religious leaders kept trying to pull fast ones over on Jesus. This tickles me because they never can. He's smarter than they are. This religious leader knew the right answers; he just didn't want to live the right life. Jesus told him if he would love God and his neighbor, he would really live. And the religious leader (Sunday school teacher?) immediately started looking for loopholes. He wanted an out. He wanted to place restrictions on who he had to love. Maybe he wanted to define who his "neighbor" was so he could check people off of his list and be done with it. He asked Jesus, "Who is my neighbor?" and Jesus took this opportunity to drive a point home. The loving of your neighbor was not found in having the right answers or caring for a certain type of people. The loving of your neighbor was not found in valuing oneself and one's work more than actual people. Just because you claimed to work for God didn't mean you acted like him. Loving your neighbor was found in the action, the response, and the mercy that was poured out. The despised Samaritan showed us what real loving is all about. The Jew's enemy had acted more compassionately than his pastor. He rearranged his own trip. He paid for this man's care out of his own pocket. He took care of this broken and bleeding Jewish man because that was what needed to be done, not because it fit neatly into his schedule. He loved him.

Our lives are so hectic because we supergirls are getting ready to do things for God, for goodness' sake. Do we really need to stop and love our kids? Our co-workers? Our sisters who borrow all of our clothes and forget to dry-clean them? Apparently, we do. If we can't love the people God has strategically placed in the middle of our path, we are totally missing the point.

What Jesus says in this parable is that loving people is what God is all about. We supergirls need to be about loving God, and we need to be about loving people. We need to love the people who can't take care of themselves. We need to love the people who are hurt and need more than a little of our time. We need to be willing to cross to the other side of the road and love people where they are. If we're not doing that, then we might as well just pack it all in. We can't do anything for God if we are not loving people.

Just so you know, the Liar hates it when we love people. It makes him cranky.

Loving people is rarely convenient. Loving people doesn't usually mesh well with our time constraints. Love is needed in moments of great adversity and discomfort, and it usually comes at our expense. That is what love is: pouring yourself out for someone else because that person is God's kid. He wants us to love our neighbor, these people he has placed in our lives and on our hearts. He would like us to take care of them because that is what he does. And I think if we tired supergirls think about it, that is what we have been wanting to do all along. Even on Sunday mornings.

Truth #15: **I need to love people . . . period.**

LIE #16

I AM IN CONTROL
OF MY DESTINY

I may not be totally sure of what exactly my destiny is, but I'm sure of one thing: I don't want anyone telling me what to do. I also do not want anyone defining me, boxing me in, giving me too much direction, or thinking they know me better than I know myself.

My husband, Scott, has seen this played out rather frequently in our marriage. Bless his heart. I am sure his heavenly mansion will have a sign over the front door that reads "Because she never listened to me." He is pretty brilliant, but I prefer to figure things out for myself rather than hear what he has to say. When blogging had just started to take off and I was struggling to get my writing noticed, Scott told me, "You should start a blog. It would be really good for your writing."

I said something really kind like, "Are you kidding? Do you see all that I have going on here with the three children? It is all I can do to break away for a smidgen of chocolate in the afternoon. I would never be able to find the time to write on a daily basis."

About a year later, I was at a writers' conference pitching a book idea, and an editor asked me, "What is your platform?"

To which I answered, "Huh?"

"Who would buy your book?"

He glanced at my proposal.

"It says here that you and your husband pastor a church. How large is your church?"

I took a moment to think how to frame my answer.

"We have a very vibrant congregation of twelve . . . twenty on a good Sunday. We're a church plant."

He was unimpressed.

"Do you have an audience? Who listens to you?"

Again I paused.

"I have three very small children who rarely listen to me, and I feel certain that none of them would buy my book. But I do go to the park a lot. I could take my books to parks with me and throw them at moms who are passing by."

Luckily, he laughed, and then he said the fateful words, "You need to start a blog. You need to build an audience. Then come back to me and pitch your book."

You need to start a blog. Where had I heard those words before? And wouldn't you know, I heard them frequently over the course of the conference as I spoke with different editors. So when I got home I whispered to Scott, "They said I need to start a blog."

"What?" he said. "I couldn't hear you."

"They said I need to start a blog."

"You know you could have started a blog a long time ago, right?"

"Yes."

"But you didn't want to do it when I told you to do it."

"I know."

"But now they are telling you that you need one, so you would like me to help you set one up?"

"Yes."

"Are you going to listen to me next time?"

"Yes."

"Promise?"

"Yes."

And lo and behold, I started blogging, and I enjoy it. Who would've known? Unfortunately, things don't fare much better in my walk with Christ. I know Jesus requires certain things of me daily if I am to be like him, like sharing others' burdens and giving him my heart. Although I know these things, I don't do these things because then I would be, you know, doing what someone else was telling me to do. And then I wouldn't be in control of my destiny.

We tired supergirls don't particularly enjoy taking direction. We like to think we have it all mapped out. We prefer to lead rather than follow. We want to live our lives on our own terms—or crash and burn on our own terms, as the case may be. Just like Eve. We would rather not heed words of wisdom (don't eat the fruit, Eve) but would like to take matters into our own hands (Eve is now eating the fruit) no matter what the consequences may be (say good-bye to the good life, Eve). But at least Eve was thrown out of the garden on her own terms, right? That sounds ridiculous, doesn't it?

This is the way of the Liar: making the ridiculous sound completely sane. We always think that we know better than God or that our lives will be better if we do our own thing.

God says, "Don't lie." And we say, "I will only lie when it really benefits me." Ever heard of a lie that panned out well?

He says, "Steer clear of temptation." And we say, "I will get as close to temptation as possible and show you how strong I am." How has that thought process worked out for us? Not well.

But the Liar really has us on this one because we like the sound of our own reasoning. He barely has to nudge us or twist the truth at all to get us thinking that we know better than God. He just says this: "You are in control of your destiny."

Then we are off and running with our own brilliant schemes . . . of self-destruction.

Judas thought he knew better than Jesus too. Take this example from when they were visiting Mary, Martha, and Lazarus:

Then Mary took a twelve-ounce jar of expensive perfume made from essence of nard, and she anointed Jesus' feet with it, wiping his feet with her hair. The house was filled with the fragrance.

But Judas Iscariot, the disciple who would soon betray him, said, "That perfume was worth a year's wages. It should have been sold and the money given to the poor." Not that he cared for the poor—he was a thief, and since he was in charge of the disciples' money, he often stole some for himself.

Jesus replied, "Leave her alone. She did this in preparation for my burial. You will always have the poor among you, but you will not always have me."

John 12:3–8

The juxtaposition in this story is amazing. Mary was pouring out her heart at the feet of Jesus. What was most precious to her, she was giving to him. She was oblivious to anything other than the fact that she wanted to give Jesus her all. And then there was Judas. He was already a bit shady in his dealings. He was taking money from the pot, and he got upset when Mary poured expensive perfume on Jesus, blessing him, rather than offering the money to go into the funds Judas was stealing from. And Jesus responded to what they both offered him. He blessed Mary, and he let Judas go his own way. Why did he let Judas go when he knew what he was going to do? It's called free will, tired supergirls. But Jesus was not above calling Judas on his stuff. I wonder if he was looking straight at Judas when he said, "You will always have the poor among you, but you will not always have me" (John 12:8).

Jesus had to know what was going on in Judas's head. He had to know the reason he would not be with them much longer was because Judas would betray him. In fact, Judas was already betraying Jesus by the way he was stealing from the pot. All Judas could think about was how he could better himself and make a little money on the side. Then he hit the jackpot: thirty pieces of silver for kissing Jesus on the cheek. Only after Jesus was taken into custody did Judas realize the full extent of what he had done. Because he wanted control of his destiny, he sold out the only one who could save him. He lost control of his destiny when he sold his soul to the devil.

Judas was shameless, wasn't he? Selling out Jesus. How could he choose to follow his own plans, his own schemes, when Jesus was right there? I don't know—how can we? We often look like Judas in the way we live our lives. He wanted to live life the way he wanted to live it. So do we. He didn't want to submit to someone else's terms. Neither do we. A bit of slippery, half-hearted truth is found in the words of the Liar: we *are* in control of our destiny, because we get to choose to whom or what we give our lives. We are giving our lives away, piece by piece, moment by moment, every day. Are we going to give our lives to the one who can save us or to the one who will crush our spirits?

We can either be like Judas, selling Jesus out one piece of silver at a time, or we can be like Mary, offering all that we have and laying all that is precious to us at his feet. We can either follow our plan or follow God's plan. From the looks of things, Mary made the better choice. Judas? Not so much. I think we should place our destiny in the hands of the one who loves us best, don't you?

Truth #16: I get to choose who I give my life to.

LIE #17
I CAN'T HEAR GOD'S VOICE

Scott always mocks me a little when I am reading. He says the house could be on fire and I wouldn't notice. I go far away into an unknown land when I read. Well, I know what land I am in. I am in whatever land the book takes place in. It's that simple. Often I come back to reality with Scott staring very intently at me.

"Did you hear anything I said?"

"Did you say something?"

"Yes, I have been talking to you for five minutes."

"Oh, I'm sorry . . . I was in seventeenth-century Scotland, high up on the heather hills with a wee breeze blowing about the bracken."

"Of course you were." Scott is always very understanding when I don't hear him at all. Or maybe he is more frustrated. I come by my inability to hear while reading honestly. It was passed down from my mom to me and my sisters, and now my son Jack is no longer with us when he reads. I see the same faraway look on his face when he is deep in the pages of a good story. Then I am the one who is frustrated, since I am usually trying to get him to pick up his room or do his homework or just look up from his book so that I can make eye contact with him. When I have asked him for the third time to put his book down, I usually start meting out consequences, like "If you don't put your book down, I am going to have to take it away from you."

Usually he does not pay any attention to me until I actually remove the book from his hands. And then, quite naturally, he is upset.

"Mom! Don't take my book! I didn't hear you. I didn't know you were talking to me!"

To which I usually respond, "I've asked you three times to put your book down. You didn't hear me because you weren't listening." Then I have this weird déjà vu flashback, because that exact same scenario played out when I was young and lost in a fog while reading a book. But my mom was clearly in the wrong when I was little. She should have spoken louder to get my attention.

Sometimes I think the same thing happens when God is trying to speak to me. I am so involved in the story that is playing out in front of me that I don't even hear what he is saying. It's not that I don't want to hear what he is saying. It's just that there are other things going on. Like life and things.

We supergirls have the tendency to get so involved in life that we don't have a clue what God is saying to us. We are doing important things, though. We are getting up early and going to work. We are working on relationships and packing lunches. We are attending home association meetings and listening to lectures on western civilization. It would be nice to hear what God had to say about our daily lives, and it would be beneficial to get a little direction from him, but at the moment we are a touch preoccupied. Just a touch.

Other times we think we may hear God speaking, but we are not sure if he is really saying what we think he is saying. Very few of us tired supergirls hear audible voices or see writing on the wall or have people speak prophetically into our lives. Mostly we are trying to make educated guesses about what he is saying. For instance, we think he wants us to love people, but we are not really sure what that entails, so we'll just go with what feels right to us. We don't really have time to pray or check in with Scripture because we are so busy living, remember? And then when God snatches our proverbial book out of our hands and our lives are turned upside down, we look around and say, "What? Was that you, God? I didn't hear what you were saying!"

The Liar gets a kick out of this, and he uses this scenario to his advantage. When we are confused about how our life is turning out, he just says, "You can't hear God. He doesn't speak to you. You are going to have to figure this out on your own."

Or, "Maybe if you had gone to more Sunday school classes when you were little, you would know how to hear him."

Or, "Obviously, God has someone else he would rather talk to. There are certain people that he talks to, like pastors and small group leaders and Beth Moore, and then there is you. You? Not so much."

Because we supergirls have been so distracted or busy or haven't really spent time trying to listen to God's voice, we think the Liar is right. It seems true. We can't hear anything. God must not be speaking.

But the truth is, God has never stopped speaking. He speaks through his creation. He speaks through his Scripture. He speaks through his people and speaks through circumstances and trials and blessings. He speaks so much that John, the disciple Jesus loved a whole lot, had a special name for Jesus. He called Jesus "the Word":

> In the beginning the Word already existed. The Word was with God, and the Word was God.
>
> John 1:1

Jesus's whole life was a message. A message of God's love. A message of God's hope. A message of reconciliation. All throughout Scripture, Old Testament and New Testament, God is looking for someone who will listen to him and respond to him. When Jesus came to earth, that message just got louder. One day Jesus was with a crowd of people, and he started telling a story about a farmer sowing seeds. This farmer threw seeds everywhere. Some landed on hard ground, some landed on rocky ground, some landed on thorny ground, and some landed on good soil. Jesus told what happened to each type of seed—some seeds thrived and some didn't. Jesus went on to explain his message to the disciples:

> You are permitted to understand the secrets of the Kingdom of Heaven, but others are not. To those who are open to my teaching, more understanding will be given, and they will have an abundance of knowledge. But for those who are not listening, even what little understanding they have will be taken away from them. That is why I use these parables,
>
> > For they look, but they don't really see.
> > They hear, but they don't really listen or understand.
>
> This fulfills the prophecy of Isaiah that says,
>
> > "When you hear what I say,
> >   you will not understand.
> > When you see what I do,
> >   you will not comprehend.
> > For the hearts of these people are hardened,
> >   and their ears cannot hear,
> > and they have closed their eyes—
> >   so their eyes cannot see,
> > and their ears cannot hear,
> >   and their hearts cannot understand,
> > and they cannot turn to me
> >   and let me heal them."

But blessed are your eyes, because they see; and your ears, because they hear. I tell you the truth, many prophets and righteous people longed to see what you see, but they didn't see it. And they longed to hear what you hear, but they didn't hear it.

Matthew 13:11–17

Apparently, we can have Jesus's message all around us and not understand a thing about it if we aren't actively listening. It sounds a bit like living life with our head stuck in a book.

Jesus went on:

Now listen to the explanation of the parable about the farmer planting seeds: The seed that fell on the footpath represents those who hear the message about the Kingdom and don't understand it. Then the evil one comes and snatches away the seed that was planted in their hearts. The seed on the rocky soil represents those who hear the message and immediately receive it with joy. But since they don't have deep roots, they don't last long. They fall away as soon as they have problems or are persecuted for believing God's word. The seed that fell among the thorns represents those who hear God's word, but all too quickly the message is crowded out by the worries of this life and the lure of wealth, so no fruit is produced. The seed that fell on good soil represents those who truly hear and understand God's word and produce a harvest of thirty, sixty, or even a hundred times as much as had been planted!

Matthew 13:18–23

The Liar would like us to be distracted from or just plain oblivious to the things God has on his heart for us. The Liar wants us to be hard or rocky or thorny soil. He prefers for God's message to wither and die inside of us. The truth is that God has designs on us to be good soil. God has not stopped trying to get his message out. He has not stopped talking to us. He has not stopped trying to get us to listen. He will use any way he can to get our attention. He will rip books out of our hands and shout down the years at us. He wants us to hear his voice. He sent his Son so we could hear his message and see his message played out in real life. Do you know what his message is? It's that he loves us. I think we should listen to him.

Truth #17: God is speaking to me.

LIE #18
I ONLY HAVE TO FORGIVE PEOPLE WHEN I FEEL LIKE IT

I am a fan of forgiveness. I think it is an amazing concept. I love that Jesus sees my mess and says, "I'm going to forgive you and take away your shame. I will take it on myself and be done with it."

This is pretty much unfathomable since I am the one in the wrong. Jesus makes the choice to restore our relationship and offer me grace with a side of mercy, despite the fact that I have hurt his heart. I hurt his heart almost every day because I sin. And every day when I say, "Jesus, I did it again. I am sorry. I want to be different," he says, "I forgive you. I want to help you be different. Let's keep working together on your life."

How can he do that? How can he be so free and so pointed with his forgiveness? I love it, but I can't comprehend it. And if we are talking about truth, and we are, the truth is I have a really hard time forgiving people, even though I know that Jesus has forgiven me.

I have this problem: I remember things. I don't remember things I am supposed to remember, like taking chocolate kisses for Will's Valentine's Day party, but I do remember how my best friend in kindergarten ditched me when we got to first grade. We had been assigned different teachers. My teacher was Mrs. Hendrix. She had the sweetest afro in all of Yankee Ridge Elementary. But my friend wasn't in my class, and as I was walking home on the first day of school, I spotted her walking ahead of me. I started running after her, calling her name, trying to catch up with her. When she heard my voice, she began to run. And she was faster than I was. That was how I learned that we weren't friends anymore. I stopped running. I still remember that stab of sorrow in my baby heart at knowing that I had been left behind. Why do I recall these things so vividly? Heart hurt does that. It has a long memory.

Now, I will say at this point that I am not harboring unforgiveness toward my best friend in kindergarten. Thankfully, I have moved on. But the knowledge that people have wronged me sits in my gut and just stays there. I know that I should forgive the people who hurt me. Jesus says to pray this way: "Forgive us our debts, as we also have forgiven our debtors" (Matt. 6:12 NIV).

But that is easier to say than it is to do. Why do I still feel this residue of unforgiveness? If I have forgiven someone, shouldn't all the bad feelings go away?

We tired supergirls want to forgive. At least we think we do. Well, what we really want to do is stop feeling so bad about all the hurtful things people have done to us over the years. We want to get rid of this stuck feeling that we can't get free of our past hurts. From kindergarten through college, people have hurt us. From work to church to family to friends, people we thought cared about us and loved us have dealt us huge blows and small wounds, and we would like to be able to get over these things; but every time we see these people, it all comes flooding back in a wave of unforgiveness. We remember that time our coworker lied and got us in trouble to save his own skin. Or the time the friend who said she would always be a friend gossiped about us behind our back. That's not even counting all the hurts involving husbands, best friends, and great-aunts. How can we forgive these things? Maybe we can't. Maybe we are incapable of forgiveness. And maybe we don't have to forgive if we don't feel like it.

The Liar agrees with us that we are incapable of forgiveness. He is a fan of unforgiveness. It is his specialty. Unforgiveness breeds a lot of other yucky by-products like jealousy, hatred, despair, judgment, condemnation, and dissension. It breaks people down and pulls them apart from each other, separating us from God, our families, our friends, and even our enemies, because if we can't forgive them, then we are alone. So the Liar encourages us in this state. He says, "Of course, you can't forgive Frances. You cry every time you think about what she said to you. You will never be the same."

Or, "I can't believe that you would even consider forgiveness. Shirley hasn't even said she was sorry. How can you forgive someone when she isn't sorry?"

Or even, "Your family will hurt you all over again if you forgive them. Might as well just get out while the getting is good. Try to protect your heart a little this time, won't you?"

But the thing the Liar forgets to mention is that if we don't forgive others, then Jesus won't forgive us. With forgiveness it is all or nothing. If we want to live free, then we have to forgive the people who have hurt us. It's our only choice. Jesus laid it out like this in a parable:

> The Kingdom of Heaven can be compared to a king who decided to bring his accounts up to date with servants who had borrowed money from him. In the process, one of his debtors was brought in who owed him millions of dollars. He couldn't pay, so his master ordered that he be sold—along with his wife, his children, and everything he owned—to pay the debt.
>
> But the man fell down before his master and begged him, "Please be patient with me, and I will pay it all." Then his master was filled with pity for him, and he released him and forgave his debt.

But when the man left the king, he went to a fellow servant who owed him a few thousand dollars. He grabbed him by the throat and demanded instant payment.

His fellow servant fell down before him and begged for a little more time. "Be patient with me, and I will pay it," he pleaded. But his creditor wouldn't wait. He had the man arrested and put in prison until the debt could be paid in full.

When some of the other servants saw this, they were very upset. They went to the king and told him everything that had happened. Then the king called in the man he had forgiven and said, "You evil servant! I forgave you that tremendous debt because you pleaded with me. Shouldn't you have mercy on your fellow servant, just as I had mercy on you?" Then the angry king sent the man to prison to be tortured until he had paid his entire debt.

Matthew 18:23–34

Then Jesus went on to tell them what this looks like in real life:

That's what my heavenly Father will do to you if you refuse to forgive your brothers and sisters from your heart.

Matthew 18:35

Here the king had set the debtor free when the debtor should have been sent to jail. Forgiveness. Then in turn, the debtor found someone who owed him money and sent him to prison. Unforgiveness. The king, who was irate at this lack of mercy, sent the debtor to prison. Prison. The debtor who was once forgiven and free was now in prison because he wouldn't forgive.

This is what we tired supergirls don't seem to understand: when we decide not to forgive the people who have hurt us, we end up in prison. By our own choosing, we do not live free. By our own choosing, we throw off mercy and embrace anger. By our own choosing, we reject grace and grab onto hatred. When we decide we can't forgive those who have hurt us most (and oh, how they have hurt us), we are choosing to walk away from the freedom of God's forgiveness and walk into a jail of our own making, where we live in loneliness and hurt. And that's not right. It is what the Liar delights in, but it is not right.

Tired supergirls everywhere long to be free from the hurt of the past. What they don't realize is that they get to make the first move. Just like Jesus reached out and forgave us first since we wronged him, we get to reach out and forgive those who have wronged us. And that seems impossible. Yes, it does. But that is where Jesus comes in, because he loves the impossible. Impossible doesn't faze him in the least. Who can help us forgive in the midst of our pain? The one who forgave the most in the midst of his pain. Jesus. Dying on the cross, pinned beneath our sins, he called out to the Father, "Forgive them! They have no idea what they are doing!" (see Luke 23:34).

He walked out forgiveness with his last breath. And he will walk it out with us. It's what he came to do, remember? He came to set the prisoners free. That is me. That is you. I think he would like to rip open some bars of unforgiveness, grab all that junk out of our arms, that junk that is piercing our hearts and hurting our souls, and throw it into the next galaxy. And then he would like to grab us up in a giant hug and say, "Let's get out of here. You're free!"

This reminds me of one of my favorite songs, "Let It Go" by singer/songwriter Lori Sabin. A supergirl in her own right, she sings about letting it go:

> Come, Lord, come
> Stay close and wash my tears away
> Fill me up 'til I'm overflowing with your grace

Then I can truly say
Relief
I can breathe
Why did it take me so long
Oh, rest!
Maybe now I can go to sleep
Relief
Lay it down
Let it go

Now is the time to let it go and break away. We know what it's like to be in prison. Let's choose to be free. Jesus will help us, tired supergirls. Freedom is what he does best. Can I get an amen?

Truth #18: **Jesus will help me forgive.**

LIE **#19**
I DON'T NEED
TO SERVE PEOPLE

A few years ago, when our church was meeting in a high school liberal arts theater, we came up against a strong attack of the enemy. He was advancing on all sides. He was trying to take us out. I am quite sure we were under a demonic stronghold by way of the bathrooms. I have never experienced such smelly bathrooms in my life. They were a bit on the filthy side as well. Maybe it was because I was pregnant and had a highly intensified sense of smell, but I don't think so. You all have witnessed high school bathrooms. They can bring even the strongest of women to their knees. We paid a cleaning crew to clean the theater and the bathrooms, but apparently the filth overwhelmed the cleaning crew. They could not break through. We would hold our noses and yell at our children lest they touch anything while they were in the bathroom. I resorted to flushing the toilet with a downward thrust of my heel applied to the flusher.

One Sunday when I was complaining about the hideousness of the bathrooms to my friend Paula, she said, "Sue, we could come early and bring some supplies and clean the bathrooms."

I was shocked and appalled and shocked. I said, "We pay for someone to clean the bathrooms. We are not cleaning the bathrooms."

Paula tends to have a servant heart toward the church. Me? Not so much. And I tend to draw the line at gross bathrooms. I hate cleaning my own bathrooms. Why would I want to clean church bathrooms? I'm not against baking some muffins for a special event, but don't expect me to be pulling out wet wipes and cleaning the urinals. I want to serve people, but really? A person has to set boundaries somewhere. Sometimes I get tired of dealing with my own family's dirt and serving my family. Let's be honest. Sometimes I get tired of serving in general. Serving people doesn't really have anything to do with serving Jesus, does it?

In case you haven't noticed, we tired supergirls are a bit worn out from serving. We serve on committees. We serve our bosses who needed those reports yesterday. We serve our kids' teachers by driving second graders on class field trips. We serve our children breakfast, lunch, and dinner, not to mention snacks, and then we serve them by washing their plates. A whole lot of serving is going on, except for the part where people serve us. So sometimes we get tired of serving and think maybe we don't need to serve people at all. Maybe somebody needs to drive *us* on a field trip. We are important too. Aren't we?

The Liar capitalizes on these sentiments. He likes that we think serving others is beneath us. This is another lie he likes to lay on thick because it serves him when we get fed up with serving each other. To show his approval, he cheers us on by saying things like, "You are absolutely right. You are worth more than this. You deserve to be served. Quit wasting your time serving others."

Or, "Don't humble yourself like that. It's embarrassing. If you serve people, they will think you can be taken advantage of."

Or, "Just don't do it anymore. Serve yourself. You are the most important."

You are the most important. This is a statement that our self-serve culture thrives on. The world should revolve around us. Our home, our work, our church, our friends, our family should serve us. Now, that sounds a little bit self-centered when it's laid out for us like that, and that's because it is. Wouldn't you know it, Jesus does not look favorably on the world being centered on us. He had some other ideas. Jesus addressed the whole "I am the most important" attitude with his followers. He actually caught the disciples arguing over who was the greatest of all of them. He called them on it. I can almost hear a chuckle in Jesus's voice as he asks, "Hey, what are you guys talking about?" No one wanted to own up to what they had been talking about. He settled the issue anyway:

> He sat down, called the twelve disciples over to him, and said, "Anyone who wants to be first must take last place and be the servant of everyone else."
>
> Mark 9:35

We don't get to hear the disciples' response to what Jesus said. Maybe they were too embarrassed to say how they felt, since they had been discussing who was the most important among them right there in God's presence. That's a bit awkward. Or maybe they were shocked over Jesus's view of who was important. The person who wanted to be first had to become a servant. The person who wanted to be the most in Jesus's eyes had to become the least. Was he for real? Yes, he was. Jesus never asked the disciples to do something he hadn't done first. His whole ministry was based on serving. He made his point again the night of the Last Supper.

Back in Jesus's day, when a guest came to your house, you washed their feet. Feet weren't pretty back then. Feet were dirty and mucky and maybe a little on the scabby side. Literally hours before he was taken into custody and led to his death, Jesus got down on the ground and washed the disciples' feet. He knew that one of the people closest to him was about to sell him out for a bit of change. He knew that he was going to be tortured and laughed at and beaten within an inch of his life. He had a few hours to tell them the most important things he could possibly tell them before he was killed, and he decided to wash his friends' feet. The story goes like this:

> Before the Passover celebration, Jesus knew that his hour had come to leave this world and return to his Father. He had loved his disciples during his ministry on earth, and now he loved them to the very end. It was time for supper, and the devil had already prompted Judas, son of Simon Iscariot, to betray Jesus. Jesus knew that the Father had given him authority over everything and that he had come from God and would return to God. So he got up from the table, took off his robe, wrapped a towel around his waist, and poured water into a basin. Then he began to wash the disciples' feet, drying them with the towel he had around him.
>
> John 13:1–5

Here is Jesus, God incarnate, washing the feet of those he created. That was the crazy love he had for them. He was willing to totally humble himself and serve the disciples because he loved them that much. This act symbolized forgiveness and love and humility and servanthood—a master washing his disciples' feet. This is the same crazy love he calls us to today. When we give our lives in service to Jesus, we are saying we give our lives in service to the ones he created, just like he did. It is the very opposite of our nature and the very essence of who Jesus was. Humility. In the smallest, most insignificant ways, we can love the people around us and bring glory to God all at the same time. When we serve, we mirror the life of the Christ. Even in the simplest of tasks. Even in the most mundane.

The Liar hates it when we love people by serving them, because then they start looking for the reason behind all this loving. "Why is she different? Why does she treat me like I am important? Why does she love me with her actions? Why does she bring cleaning wipes to the theater and wipe down the bathrooms before the service starts?"

And we tired supergirls can say this: "Because of Jesus. He wanted me to show his love to you."

When we serve our friends, our coworkers, and our families, we are showing them the extent of Jesus's love—a Creator God humbling himself to serve his creation. Washing feet. Doing dishes. Driving on field trips. Let's let the love flow. Even if that means cleaning church bathrooms.

Truth #19: When I serve people, I am like Jesus.

LIE **#20**

I NEED TO BE GOOD SO THAT GOD WILL LOVE ME

As a child I was well acquainted with spankings and with spending copious amounts of time in my room. My mom always called me a "curious" child. Scott says that means that I was a terror. I don't know if I was a terror, but I was often in trouble. Despite my rambunctious ways, I did have a healthy fear of discipline. I guess it just wasn't healthy enough to keep me out of trouble. But I was always loath to hear the words "Just wait until your dad gets home."

None of us four kids ever wanted to hear those words. This was the bomb our mom dropped on us after we had tried her very last nerve. It meant she was done with us and our craziness. It meant Mom was going to hold off on the punishment until the big guns got home. This phrase struck fear into our hearts. When Dad pulled into the driveway, we would scatter, but Mom never forgot her promise. Dad would call us into the house, and let's just say we were dealt with accordingly for hitting each other, for breaking each others' toys, for pulling hair and calling names and bugging each other to no end. We never doubted that there would be consequences for our actions. Mom and Dad were consistent in letting us know that there was a good way to behave and a not-so-good way to behave. And we tested those limits over and over. We would find out, "Yep, I still get in trouble when I smack someone on the back of the head, even if it looks real funny when their head snaps forward."

One thing was for sure: I didn't need anyone to tell me when I was being good or not good. I knew that right off. I knew in my gut the difference between good and not good. And mostly? I was not good.

Things are not so different in my relationship with God. I am still very aware of the difference between good and not good. And most of the time, I know I've got a whole lot of not good going on. The scary part is that now, as an adult, I realize that God is holy. And if you want to be in the presence of a holy God, then you also have to be holy. In case you didn't realize it, let me tell you, it's very hard to be holy when you've got a whole lot of not good going on. I know this because I have gone to Sunday school and youth group and college class and young-married class and big church, but no matter how much grace I've heard preached, in the back of my mind I often equate God's love and his acceptance of me with my ability to stay on the straight and narrow. I have a secret terrifying fear that if I really mess up terribly, I will hear Jesus call out across the cosmos, "Just wait until my Dad gets home!" I have this undeniable inkling that a divine smackdown will be waiting for me.

So a lot of times I am motivated to live a good life not out of love for God but out of an unhealthy fear of him. Love doesn't exactly flourish in the presence of fear. But striving does. So I strive to be really good, since maybe he only loves those giants of the faith who have conquered their issues and are living powerful lives for God. Even though I am not good at the core, I try to pack my life with goodness by doing good things so that Jesus will love me. I follow all his rules the best I can. I go to church (I have to—it's part of my job description as a pastor's wife). I even sing on the worship team occasionally. That's got to earn me some points, doesn't it?

We tired supergirls try really hard to be good. And we try really hard to do good. We try to live right and love people and not get angry when our best shirt is ruined by a crayon in the dryer. We try not to yell at people who cut us off. We try to live free and help people in need and go to all of the small group activities that are required of us. We really try to be forgiving and give our time to worthwhile things like mission trips, and we shop only in the sale section because we are good stewards. But it is really hard to be good. Really hard. In fact, if we have to be good for God to love us, we may not make it, because just last Thursday we thought bad thoughts about another supergirl and wanted to kick her right in the shins when she humiliated us in front of our friends. We are very aware we are not good, even though we refrained from the shin kicking.

The Liar loves to spread this lie that we have to be good for God to love us on extra thick with extra lie power on top. He is extremely fond of this lie. It's his favorite. You know why? Because if the Liar can get us to believe this, then he can convince us that God will never really love us. Those of us who already have doubts in this area are easy targets, since we can't seem to get past the fact that we have a whole lot of not good going on. Once we think our salvation is based on our goodness, we are sunk. The Liar keeps us distracted from the truth by yelling at us, "Just in case you forgot, you are lousy!"

Or, "God is so incredibly ticked off by you. How many times have you disobeyed him? Shameless."

Or, and he really likes this one, "Try harder. Maybe you will be good enough next week."

In Jesus's day a group of people kept trying to impress God with their goodness. They were involved in their churches, they lived holy lives, and they followed all the rules. I think they probably sang on their worship teams. Do you know who they were? The Pharisees. The do-gooders. They were so good that they even told people they were good. They thought their goodness earned them God's love. His acceptance. His favor. They were so caught up in earning God's love and acceptance and favor that they missed the fact that God's love was standing right in front of them in the person of Jesus.

Then there was the other group of people back in Jesus's day. These were the ones Jesus spent most of his time with. I know this might shock you. It definitely shocked the Pharisees. He spent a majority of his time with people who were no good at all. He hung out with people who weren't even trying to be good. They just let their sins hang out there in the open. Tax collectors. Swindlers. Liars. Thieves. Rebels. Ladies with tainted reputations. Jesus surrounded himself with the people who needed him the most: sinners. And you know what is even more shocking? Jesus loved them just the way they were, even before they started trying to be good.

One thief hanging on the cross next to Jesus figured it out (see Luke 23:32–43). I don't know how he did, but he did. Somehow he realized that he had no goodness of his own to offer God, but he was hoping Jesus would love him anyway. On the darkest day in history, bleeding and gasping for breath, this thief, who is no good, asks Jesus, who is goodness incarnate, to remember him. Just to remember him when he comes into his kingdom. Now, this thief knows he doesn't have a chance to even try to be good. He is dying, for goodness' sake. He will never be able to make up for his wrongdoing. But he is wondering: if he believes who Jesus says he is, the Christ, the Son of the Living God, is that enough?

Yes, tired supergirls, it is. Paul tells us the truth in Romans: "But God showed his great love for us by sending Christ to die for us while we were still sinners" (5:8).

We limit God's ability to work in us when we choose to earn God's love rather than accept it for free. We limit our own ability to love God, to throw ourselves on his mercy, to bare our souls to him, when we buy into the lie that we have to be good for God to love us. If we think we have the ability to merit God's love by our goodness, we become like the Pharisees back in Jesus's day. They were doing all the right things with the wrong heart. The right heart realizes that it's not about our ability to be good; it's about Jesus's great love for us. The right heart realizes that we will never be good enough to achieve God's love, but the right heart asks for it anyway. The right heart is the one that says, "Lord, I'm dying over here. I've got nothing to offer you. Nothing. Will you love me anyway?" and he says, "Done."

It is finished. With his last breath he closed the gap between us and his Father. The gap that said we weren't holy so we couldn't be in his presence. The gap that said we were no good. We don't have to be afraid anymore. We don't have to have any more striving or trying or aching to be good. I can almost hear Jesus shouting out across the cosmos, "We can't wait until *you* get home!"

And tired supergirls, it just doesn't get any better than that.

Truth #20: God loves me even when I'm not good.

LIE **#21**
I DON'T NEED TO CHANGE

Three years ago I had my last baby, Addison. I have passed by this season in a semi-fog, and I cannot believe my baby can now get himself a drink of water from the sink if he wants to. It amazes me. I look at him and think, "He was such a little bundle of chub-i-licious-ness! And now he's so big. He can ask for chocolate outright! That's my boy!"

Unfortunately, only one of us has any claim on chub-i-licious-ness at this point. That would be me. My stomach has never quite returned to its normal state. This could be due to the fact that Addison weighed nine pounds twelve ounces at birth. Or it could be due to the fact that I can also ask for chocolate outright, and I often just go to the cupboard and help myself. I have often lamented the fact that my belly button is no longer shaped like a circle but folds over into a frown. Just the other day my son Will caught sight of it and said, "Wow, Mom! Your belly button really goes far in."

He was a little amazed by its depth, and to be honest, so am I. No one wants a belly button that can hold water. It's just not pretty. I don't even remember what my pre-Addison belly looked like, but I do know it didn't look like this. I have decided I am fed up with this belly. But how does one begin to reform one's stomach muscles? My stomach muscles have been lax for years. I know I must take drastic measures to change the shape of my belly button that frowns at me. What I wouldn't give for a belly button shaped in a round O of surprise. That would be something, wouldn't it, if one morning I woke up with a flat, nongelatinous belly? It would pretty much be miraculous since I hate exercising.

In the back of my mind, I know that one thing that can change my belly: exercise. I used to be a mean sit-up machine back in the third grade, but things have slipped a bit since then. I'm almost convinced that my core muscles have vacated the premises. To bring them back means I have to do crunches and sit-ups and bicycle kicks and all the things one does to tone and flatten and strengthen one's stomach muscles. And wouldn't you know it, it kind of hurts to do those things over and over. I know this because recently my sisters and I have started doing an exercise video that makes us do all those things. We email each other and say mean things about the girls on the videos with their spandex and trim waists. Then we bemoan the fact that we are so sore. Who knew we could be so sore? And then I start to think things like maybe a frowning belly button is not the worst thing in the world to have, and maybe an alternate way to build up bone density, other than weight-bearing exercise, is to eat chocolate-covered cookies on my couch since there is calcium in the chocolate. Isn't there calcium in chocolate? But the point is, maybe I don't need to change. Maybe I am fine exactly the way I am.

Tired supergirls everywhere would like to not change. We would like to stay the way we are because really, change taxes us too much. Maybe we don't need to get out of the bad relationship with the jerky guy, because we have poured a lot of our heart into that jerky guy and we don't want to walk away from that part of our heart. He's a bad habit, but he is our bad habit. It's too hard to leave. And maybe we don't need to clean up our language and put a lid on the gossip and cattiness, because who is listening anyway? It's too hard to pay attention to what we say. And maybe we supergirls don't need to stop yelling at our kids. They are wild, after all, and the only way to get their attention is by screeching. It would be too hard to try to reframe our words in a positive way. And while we are at it, who really needs core muscles? We were always fond of our grandma with osteoporosis. It can't be that bad to be bent over. It's just too hard to change . . . so let's not.

The Liar has a great line that he feeds us about change. When God has pinpointed an area that we supergirls need to change, the Liar likes to say, "You are fine just the way you are." It's so nice of him to say that, isn't it?

And then he further comforts us with this thought: "You don't need to change." He is so sweet, isn't he?

And then he rounds it out by saying, "Don't do anything that is too hard for you. You should take it easy."

We love this lie. We think this Liar is okay. He is really a swell guy. The thing we don't hear is that he is also muttering under his breath, "Let's keep you stuck right where you are. Why don't you go nowhere with me?" (evil chuckle follows).

Let's just say this outright: the lies of the enemy are just that. They are lies of someone who is against us. He will never be on our side. Ever. He would like to destroy us. He will do it any way he can. When he is encouraging us to never change, he is flying in the face of everything that Jesus embraces. Jesus loves change. He loves darkness becoming light. He loves death becoming life. He loves blindness becoming sight. He loves deafness becoming hearing. Change equals growth. And if there is anything Jesus is for, it is growth. Transformation. Liberation. Salvation. All those good "tion" words embrace change. And wouldn't you know it, supergirls—if we want to be like Jesus, we are going to have to change. The Liar would like us to focus on the painful part of this process, the stretching and the discomfort and the plodding parts of change. But Jesus wants us to look past the pain to the end result. He wants us to focus on a life that mirrors his. Paul talks about it this way:

> Don't copy the behavior and customs of the world, but let God transform you into a new person by changing the way you think. Then you will know God's will for you, which is good and pleasing and perfect.
>
> Romans 12:2

And again in Colossians 3:8–10:

> But now is the time to get rid of anger, rage, malicious behavior, slander, and dirty language. Don't lie to each other, for you have stripped off your old sinful nature and all its wicked deeds. Put on your new nature, and be renewed as you learn to know your Creator and become like him.

The Liar would like us to stay the way we are—in our old ways, our old habits, our same old, same old. But Jesus would like us to become like him. He didn't die on the cross so we could keep on living the way we have always lived. He died so we could be transformed. He died so we could have a new life, and a life touched by his glory at that. He died so that we could live like him, talk like him, bless people like him, and touch the world like he did, and that is not going to happen if we stay stuck in our old ways. We need to change.

Paul says to let our way of thinking be completely changed. I am thinking that can only happen when we soak up a new way of thinking. Lucky for us, when Jesus left he didn't just say, "Hope you can change on your own. Good luck! It could get tricky!"

Or, "Figure it out and get back to me. Let me know how the change is going."

He sent his Holy Spirit to be with us. We are not on our own. We can change because God fills us with his Spirit. And in the midst of all the changing, the growing, the soreness, he is our Comforter. As we are cleaning up our language and toning down the screeching and doing some sit-ups, he is moving in our hearts and changing the way we see things and the way we do things. Because that is what this life of following Jesus is all about—transformation.

As we lean into him, as we read his words and listen for his voice, we begin to look like him. We begin to be shaped by his love, his joy, his peace. We really like his peace. Wouldn't you know it, we start showing signs of faithfulness and gentleness and—be still our beating hearts—some self-control. We didn't see many signs of faithfulness before, and we never thought we would have self-control, but here it is welling up within us. You know what it means, don't you? We are changing, from everlasting to everlasting, until we are exactly the supergirl we were designed to be. And it's all because of who he is in us. That is something we can smile about, supergirls, even when our stomachs are sore.

Truth #21: Jesus is changing me.

LIE **#22**
I DON'T
NEED PEOPLE

I have passed on a number of qualities to my children. Jack has my large eyes. Will has my affinity for a funky beat. Addison likes to go places. If someone, anyone, is headed out the door, he is asking to go along. And they seem to have inherited some of my not-so-stellar qualities as well, like my perfectionism and my propensity toward procrastination and my inability to remember the location of very important items like money or candy. Now, sometimes seeing one's qualities acted out by one's children is endearing. When Will busts out into a full karaoke routine with choreographed dance moves, that brings my heart some joy. But sometimes seeing one's qualities portrayed so terribly by one's offspring is horrifying.

For example, sometimes they act out my "I can do it myself" routine. This routine is fast friends with my "I don't need anyone to help me" attitude, and it has a lovely sidekick called "Leave me alone." You know, that one. It is one of my most prolific qualities. I have seen it show up in each of my children right around the age of two, even though they have barely learned to walk. They would rather not listen to the sage wisdom of their parents but prefer to pull the cat's whiskers or try to stand on a basketball without circus training or taste the unsweetened baking chocolate because "they can do it themselves." Now, you would think that you would grow out of this, say, by the age of ten after a whole bunch of "I can do it myself" disasters. But sadly, this is not the case. I still find myself flaunting this attitude on a regular basis.

When a lot of commitments come my way, when I'm faced with a dilemma, or when I am too sure of my own abilities, I simply think, "I can do this on my own. I don't need to involve someone else. It will just make it more complicated. I've got this."

This is what I think pretty much all the time about my life, except in the case of laundry. I will take all comers who want to help out with my laundry. But my "I can do it myself" attitude plays out frequently in my dealings with people at church, with Scott when we disagree about something, and with my kids when I can't get them to see things my way. I think, "Involving people in my life just gets so messy. I would rather maintain control of the outcome. It's prettier that way."

Part of this "I can do it myself" attitude is cultural, I think. As westerners, we have this feeling that to succeed in life you simply need to pull yourself up by your bootstraps and go for it. To be a "self-made" man or woman is a high accolade. We supergirls look favorably on those who beat the odds and make their own dreams come true despite obstacles or hardship. We won't let anyone or anything hold us back or stand in our way. We tired supergirls are supposed to "take the bull by the horns." But while there is nothing wrong with taking the initiative, we often end up missing the point—the point of how we are supposed to live and work and walk out this grace that God has so graciously given us.

The Liar is all over this. He would much rather us supergirls be on our own than sharing our lives with those who could build us up or strengthen us. He prefers that we stay the "I can do it myself" course in our personal lives, our work lives, and our spiritual lives. You see, it is much easier for him to get in our heads when we don't have other people around us telling us the truth. He encourages this behavior, saying things like, "You know, you really are smart. You don't need anyone to help you on this project. If you involve other people, they may disagree with you. You are much more efficient on your own."

Or, "If you invite people into this area of your life, you will make yourself way too vulnerable. You'll lose your ability to be in control. Just keep your life to yourself and everything will work out."

Or, "You don't need other people. God has given you everything you need without anyone else. You could run this ministry (or family, campaign, after-school program, lunch meeting, knitting class, Sunday school fair, sporting event, small group, marriage, friendship, walk with God, etc.) by yourself, with your eyes closed and your hands tied behind your back. Relax. You . . . don't . . . need . . . anyone."

The Liar is so very happy that we supergirls buy into this. We are, after all, supergirls. We can *totally* handle things on our own. Or not. Maybe we can't handle things on our own because we were never meant to live our lives alone. We were made in the image of our Creator. We were made for relationship. The Father, the Son, *and* the Holy Spirit. Adam *and* Eve. Moses *and* Aaron. Jesus *and* his disciples. We tired supergirls were designed with others in mind. Our friends. Our families. Our coworkers. Our baristas at Starbucks. We really need each other. We can't live the life that God designed for us alone. We can't be all that God created us to be without the influence of others. We can't make it through the innumerable trials of this life without the people God has put in our path to speak truth to us, to encourage us, and to help disciple us. We were not made to walk this journey alone.

On a spiritual level, Paul took this to heart in his own life. His missionary journeys always included others. Paul and

Barnabas. Paul and Silas. Paul and Timothy. He got that partnering with others was a good thing. He talked about this when he talked about the church and the body of Christ. He talked about the gifts that had been handed out to the believers and the ways these gifts benefitted each other:

> But our bodies have many parts, and God has put each part just where he wants it. How strange a body would be if it had only one part! Yes, there are many parts, but only one body. The eye can never say to the hand, "I don't need you." The head can't say to the feet, "I don't need you."
>
> In fact, some of the parts that seem weakest and least important are really the most necessary. And the parts we regard as less honorable are those we clothe with the greatest care. So we carefully protect those parts that should not be seen, while the more honorable parts do not require this special care. So God has put the body together such that extra honor and care are given to those parts that have less dignity. This makes for harmony among the members, so that all the members care for each other. If one part suffers, all the parts suffer with it, and if one part is honored, all the parts are glad.
>
> 1 Corinthians 12:18–26

Now, I feel very strongly that I have gone through certain seasons of being an armpit in the body of Christ. I can't claim for certain that this is true; I'm just saying that it is not always pleasant being where God puts us and doing what God has designed us to do. But the point of this passage is that we need each other. We can't function alone. Now, we would all like to be visionaries and see things, but what is God going to do with a roomful of eyeballs? Creepy. Each body part complements the other. Two situations have to be addressed here: we supergirls can not go down this road alone, and surprisingly enough, the other members of our body can not go down it without us either. When we choose to do things the "I want to do it myself" way, not only do we shut others out from being in our lives, but we keep ourselves from being in theirs. What good is an eyeball on its own—or even an armpit for that matter?

God has designed us to be woven into the fabric of each other's lives. For better or for worse. So that we can lift each other up and laugh at each other's jokes. So that we can work on projects together and pray for each other's peace of mind. So that we can share in life's sorrows and celebrate its joys. So that we can hold each other's babies and clean out each other's closets. We supergirls can be who God wants us to be in part because those who surround us are cheering us on, offering their gifts to us, and serving us as we do the same for them. The thought of all this togetherness really chaps the Liar's hide. It should. Things are starting to get good.

Truth #22: **I need the body of Christ.**

LIE #23
I AM NEVER
GOING TO GET FREE

Just yesterday, a group of us went over to my friend Georgianna's house for tea, and as we walked in, we were surrounded by a sense of calm. Candles were lit. The floors were swept. Everything was in its place. It was so very clean. Something deep within me responds to clean. I love clean. Now, you would not know this if you walked into my house, because my house is mostly—and oh, how it pains me to say this—not clean.

It has brief moments of clean. Nanoseconds of clean. But mine is a house of perpetual motion. When I clean, my children unclean within seconds. So sometimes I boycott cleaning. But when I came home from Georgianna's house last night and saw an entire bag of chips ground into our carpet, I whipped out the vacuum. Scott raised an eyebrow at me. Vacuuming midweek? Really?

"Is someone coming over?" he asked.

"No."

"Oh, because you are vacuuming."

"There was a mound of chips in the carpet."

"Oh."

Scott knows that at times I give up the good fight. I surrender to the madness and lose the will to fight for a clean house and a vacuumed carpet. When Jack, my oldest, was a baby, I had all of his toys in matching bins, labeled and stacked neatly in his closet. Now with Addison, who was baby number three, rounding the corner on toddlerhood, I just dig under the couch to find matchbox cars for him to play with.

I usually come up with a few bonus Legos for him too. He's pleased. It's gone downhill, supergirls; it really has.

But here is the thing: there are three of them and one of me. I can mop and sweep and do laundry and fold T-shirts and vacuum and scrub bathtubs, and two days later it looks like I have done nothing. *Nothing.* So what's the point? It's like trying to hold back the tide. Sometimes it just makes me howl. That really frightens Scott and the children, so I try to do it when I am alone. Every once in a while I yell out, "I just washed this red shirt yesterday!"

Or, "The cleaning never ends! Why doesn't it end?"

And then I usually end with a really uplifting thought like, "It's never going to change."

I get so tired of being stuck. Stuck in the same circumstances. The same house. The same mess. The same piles of laundry. The same muck on the floor with the same dirt ring in the bathtub. And even worse, the feeling of being stuck in an endless cycle pretty much mirrors how I feel a whole lot on the inside too. My walk with Jesus seems no different. Sometimes I feel like I am reliving the same issues, the same problems, the same muck, day in and day out with my journey of faith and all of my struggles. The difference is I am yelling different things, like: "I just forgave them yesterday!"

And, "Why can't I get past this thing? *Come on!*"

And of course, the nice finishing touch, "I'm never going to change."

All of us tired supergirls have things we struggle with over and over again, whether it is anger, overeating, lust, gossiping, or complaining about how our house is never clean. We deal with the same situations endlessly, whether it's finances, really bad choices in guys, stress management, or chafing under a really cranky boss. Just like the laundry, we seem to keep coming up against that same red shirt over and over again.

Didn't we just deal with that yesterday? Didn't we pray about this last week? Haven't we battled with this year in and year out? Can't we tired supergirls get a break? Can't we be done with this? Enough, already!

The Liar joys in our despair. He really does. He confirms our worst fears and tries to shut out any light of the truth from getting into our hearts. He doesn't have to be elaborate. He takes us out with small pointed sentences like, "You will never change."

Or, "You are the same person you were last February."

Or, "This will always be a problem for you. Get used to it."

And we believe him. We give up. We don't particularly like whatever it is that we keep coming up against, but we are pretty sure we are stuck here for life, and we are just too tired to fight it anymore. We want it to be different, but we're just not sure it ever will be, so why keep fighting?

A man in Gerasenes knew that well. He was dealing with his own demons. Literally. The story goes like this:

> So they arrived in the region of the Gerasenes, across the lake from Galilee. As Jesus was climbing out of the boat, a man who was possessed by demons came out to meet him. For a long time he had been homeless and naked, living in a cemetery outside the town.
>
> As soon as he saw Jesus, he shrieked and fell down in front of him. Then he screamed, "Why are you interfering with me, Jesus, Son of the Most High God? Please, I beg you, don't torture me!" For Jesus had already commanded the evil spirit to come out of him. This spirit had often taken control of the man. Even when he was placed under guard and put in chains and shackles, he simply broke them and rushed out into the wilderness, completely under the demon's power.
>
> Jesus demanded, "What is your name?"

172

"Legion," he replied, for he was filled with many demons. The demons kept begging Jesus not to send them into the bottomless pit.

There happened to be a large herd of pigs feeding on the hillside nearby, and the demons begged him to let them enter into the pigs.

So Jesus gave them permission. Then the demons came out of the man and entered the pigs, and the entire herd plunged down the steep hillside into the lake and drowned.

When the herdsmen saw it, they fled to the nearby town and the surrounding countryside, spreading the news as they ran. People rushed out to see what had happened. A crowd soon gathered around Jesus, and they saw the man who had been freed from the demons. He was sitting at Jesus' feet, fully clothed and perfectly sane, and they were all afraid.

Luke 8:26–35

Now, here was a man who had lived the ins and outs of despair. His days played out the same over and over again. He was so tormented that he had not worn clothes or lived in a house "for a long time" (v. 27). I wonder how long a long time is. One year? Ten years? Many times these spirits had seized him. The spirits were so powerful, so terrible, so vengeful they would cause him to break through chains and would drive him away from other people over and over. They had serious power over this man. I am sure the people in the village were totally freaked out by this guy. I would be. A naked, demon-possessed man living in a graveyard? That is scary. Demons are scary. Naked crazy people are scary.

But do you know who both the demons and the townspeople were scared of? Jesus. The demons were scared of Jesus because they knew who got to win when he was around. The townspeople had started out scared of the naked crazy guy, but now they were even more petrified of Jesus. Who had that kind of power? Here was a man who could turn back insanity. Here was someone who put the underworld in its place. He was that imposing and forceful. With a word, he silenced a legion of demons and set a man free, a man who for years hadn't had a moment's peace. With that, he put some clothes on, took a deep breath, and sat down at the feet of the one who set him free. He would never be in chains again. That was some crazy power. No wonder the people were scared. They should have been. Our Savior is powerful. Can I get an amen?

So, supergirls, here we are in our endless cycle. The Liar is shrieking in the background, trying to distract us. He really would prefer that we didn't know this truth: that he is absolutely terrified of the power of the living God. Whether laundry or jealousy or fear or a mind-numbing addiction has us dead to rights, only one person has enough power to set us free. Even if we are fighting something that has been our life for years. Even if we have thought we were done with this thing and here it comes again. We have been humbled by our struggle, feeling dead in it, too tired to fight, and wondering if we will ever be free. And here is the truth of the matter. By his word, we can be. By his power, we will be. He promises us. Remember? That is what he is all about. He died so we didn't have to die anymore. Let's believe that. Let's live it.

Truth #23: The one the Son sets free is free indeed.

conclusion

I have always thought that the saying "Liar, liar, pants on fire" was quite apropos, seeing that maybe the greatest Liar of all is found in a fiery pit. I believe his pants may very well be on fire. He is pretty tricky and evil. He deserves eternity in the hot seat. One of his best tricks ever is to get us to live out our lives in half truth or partial truth or twisted truth. It's genius, really. Because unless we know the real Truth, we may never recognize the lies for what they are: a sham, a farce, just a whole lot of worthless lines. Unless we have spent time with the real Truth, we could easily be taken in by the fake truth, because they kind of resemble each other.

It's a lot like that part in the movie *Elf* when Will Ferrell's character, an elf named Buddy, realizes that the Santa in the department store is not the real Santa, just some chubby guy with a beard. He knows this because he knows the real Santa. He's spent time with the real Santa, and the real Santa knows him by name. And as far as he recollects, the real Santa does not smell like beef and cheese, and this fake Santa smells a lot like a deli. I'm assuming the real Santa had a Santa-type smell—maybe a little milk and cookies with some North Pole thrown in. So Buddy the Elf leans over and tells the guy, "You sit on a throne of lies." And then he proceeds to rip fake Santa's beard off. He is not taken in, and he doesn't want anyone else to be taken in either. He is going to expose the impostor for who he is.

God's truth has a certain smell to it. A free smell. It smacks of grace and peace and maybe a little bit of conviction. It has the scent of forgiveness and of hope and of the eternal. And this book is about ripping off the beard of some really stinky half-truths. It is about exposing the Liar for who he is: an impostor, a poseur, a fake. All the Liar has to offer us is a really poor imitation of God's truth. If we aren't acquainted with God or his truth or the way he works, we easily buy into the Liar's rhetoric. During a talk with the Pharisees, when Jesus is calling them on all their stuff, he tells us what the Liar is all about:

> For you are the children of your father the devil, and you love to do the evil things he does. He was a murderer from the beginning. He has always hated the truth, because there is no truth in him. When he lies, it is consistent with his character; for he is a liar and the father of lies.
>
> John 8:44

I'm pretty sure that talk didn't go over that well with the Pharisees, being called children of the devil and all, but the point is, the Liar is around, and he is up to no good. In fact, he is so good at lying that he almost has us convinced of the lie that there is no Liar and all the thoughts and beliefs in our heads are really the truth. The sheer audacity he has! The only way we tired supergirls can know the real truth is by spending time with Jesus. By reading his words. By learning his teachings. By listening for his voice.

And in our heart of hearts, we tired supergirls long for the truth. That is what brought us to Jesus in the first place. We want to know how to live by the truth. We want to recognize it, and we want it to call out to us. We want its light to fill us up and spill over onto everyone around us. And more than anything, we would like it to set us free. And Jesus promises us that will happen.

> Jesus said to the people who believed in him, "You are truly my disciples if you remain faithful to my teachings. And you will know the truth, and the truth will set you free."
>
> John 8:31–32

So what does this mean for us in this journey of truth? What does this mean for us as we struggle to unearth the half-truths of the Liar? As we stare at our poorly cut bangs and own up to the fact that sometimes it is easier to believe his lies than the truth? How do we search out the truth and get past the lies of the enemy? What it means is that it's time for us supergirls to get serious. We don't wear spandex for nothing. Okay, maybe we have never worn spandex and never will, but the deal is, if we want to know the truth, we are going to have to fight for it. We are going to have to chase it down in our high-heeled boots and do some damage to the crazy lies that fill our heads. We are going to have to let loose with flying kicks and a flurry of karate chops (even get out the nunchucks if you must) when the lies sound too much like the truth, and we are going to need to help our fellow supergirls out when they are struggling. Don't be afraid to speak the truth right out, saying things like, "I know God loves me no matter what!"

And, "I may not be able to change myself, but Jesus can change me."

Or, "Hey, Liar! You stink!" Sometimes it feels good to tell the Liar he stinks. Because he does. He's rotten. Yelling it out loud may scare your roommate, though, so try to do that one when you are alone.

The Liar is going to try to take you out with his slick words and wormy lies, but you have a secret weapon. That weapon is that you are not alone. You never have been and you never will be. And you can be certain that if the Liar is trying to take you down with his slippery words, Jesus will be shouting out the truth. More than anything else, Jesus wants you to know the truth. And he is on your side. So take heart and listen to what Paul told the Ephesians:

> A final word: Be strong in the Lord and in his mighty power. Put on all of God's armor so that you will be able to stand firm against all strategies of the devil. For we are not fighting against flesh-and-blood enemies, but against evil rulers and authorities of the unseen world, against mighty powers in this dark world, and against evil spirits in the heavenly places.
>
> Therefore, put on every piece of God's armor so you will be able to resist the enemy in the time of evil. Then after the battle you will still be standing firm. Stand your ground, putting on the belt of truth and the body armor of God's righteousness. For shoes, put on the peace that comes from the Good News so that you will be fully prepared. In addition to all of these, hold up the shield of faith to stop the fiery arrows of the devil. Put on salvation as your helmet, and take the sword of the Spirit, which is the word of God.
>
> Ephesians 6:10–17

Fight on, tired supergirls, and stand firm! May you take out the Liar with a sweet roundhouse kick the next time he comes calling. Or just whack him over the head with the Bible—that works too. May the Lord fill you with his strength and shine the light of his truth on your very souls. Amen.

study questions

Lie #1: God Is Out to Get Me

1. Do you view God as the hard taskmaster or the Good Shepherd?
2. What is one situation when you thought God was going to smoke you?
3. Do you recognize the fact that Jesus wants to shepherd you?
4. How does the truth make you feel—to know that he is chasing you down with his love?

Lie #2: God Is Disappointed in Me

1. Do you feel like you disappoint God? Why?
2. What miracles has God done in your life up to this point?
3. What keeps you from believing that God is in control of the storms in your life?

4. How does the truth that God is more concerned about your ability to believe in him than your ability to be perfect affect you?

Lie #3: I Can't Be Real with God

1. Are you real with God?
2. If you were to write a psalm to the Lord at this moment, what would it say?
3. How does the truth that God wants us to be real with him change your view of him?

Lie #4: God Doesn't Have Good Plans for My Life

1. What plans do you have for your life?
2. Has God done anything recently to upend your plans?
3. What was your response to God?
4. How can the truth that God works in the mess of our lives be walked out in your life?

Lie #5: God Will Ask Me to Do Things I Don't Want to Do

1. What are you afraid of?
2. What would your life look like if you chose not to follow Jesus?
3. How could the truth that Jesus calls us to follow him in spite of our fear revolutionize the way you live?

Lie #6: God Can't Use Me

1. What do you think makes you unusable?
2. Do you identify with Peter in all of his mess-ups?
3. How does the truth that God changed Peter and used him change how you view your own usability?
4. How can you get yourself ready for God to use you?

Lie #7: God Doesn't Hear Me

1. Why do you think that God doesn't hear you?
2. How does the way you view prayer differ from how Jesus viewed prayer?
3. Will the truth that God hears you change what you say to him? How?

Lie #8: God Can't Possibly Care about Me

1. Are there any ways in your life that you feel overlooked by God?
2. What do you see in the story of Jesus feeding the five thousand that shows his heart for people?
3. How does his caring heart affect the way he interacts with us in our everyday lives?
4. Does the knowledge of his care change how you interact with him?

Lie #9: God Caused My Problems

1. What are some problems in your life that you have blamed God for?

2. Have you ever felt the way Mary and Martha did when they felt Jesus came too late to help them?
3. When has God shown up in your life and changed the outcome of your story?
4. What does the truth that God is the same today as he was in Mary and Martha's day mean to you?

Lie #10: God Doesn't Know Me

1. What keeps you from believing that God knows you inside and out?
2. If you could tell God one thing about yourself, face-to-face, what would it be?
3. Would you respond like Peter and Nathanael if you could comprehend that God knows your name and your whereabouts?
4. Does the truth that God knows the intimate details of your life make you want change how you live?

Lie #11: God Owes Me

1. What do you feel entitled to?
2. Are there any ways you feel like God has ripped you off?
3. What do you feel you owe God? Why?
4. Does knowing that God gave you his all in the person of Jesus change what you feel entitled to?

Lie #12: God Doesn't Care If I Am Thankful

1. What was the last prayer God answered for you?
2. Did you thank him for it?

3. What is something you are truly thankful for right now?

4. Does the truth that God cares about how you respond to his provision make you want to talk to God differently?

Lie #13: God Doesn't Feel Things Like I Do

1. What are you feeling right now that you wish God felt?

2. Does your perception of God change when you realize he never had to feel the way we feel but he chose to anyway?

3. How can the truth that Jesus felt everything you feel impact the way you interact with him?

Lie #14: I Will Never Be Enough

1. What are the ways you feel "less than" in your life?

2. What are the ways you feel "more than" in your life?

3. What do you think of Paul's view of his own less-than-ness? What about how he views his more-than-ness?

4. How can you apply the truth that God's grace is enough for you in real, everyday living?

Lie #15: I Can Love People at My Convenience

1. When do you find it easiest to love people? Hardest?

2. What is your response when someone else's needs interrupt your plans?

3. Do you find yourself to be more like the priest or the Good Samaritan?

4. How does the truth that God loves even in the most inconvenient of times shed light on how he wants us to love?

Lie #16: I Am in Control of My Destiny

1. Why is it so easy to follow in Eve's footsteps?
2. When do you feel the most in control of your life?
3. How do you feel when you think about handing over your destiny to God?
4. What truth from this chapter about your destiny stands out to you?

Lie #17: I Can't Hear God's Voice

1. How do you listen for God's voice?
2. In what ways has he spoken to you in the past?
3. What kind of soil do you think your heart is at the moment?
4. How does the truth that God has never stopped speaking to you affect the way you listen for his voice?

Lie #18: I Only Have to Forgive People When I Feel Like It

1. Who do you need to forgive that you haven't?
2. What caught your attention the most in the story about the king and the debtor?
3. How does the truth that your ability to forgive is linked with your ability to be forgiven affect your view of forgiveness?

Lie #19: I Don't Need to Serve People

1. What does servanthood mean to you?
2. How would you have reacted as a disciple if Jesus washed your feet?
3. How does the way Jesus lived his life in service to others inspire you?
4. How does the idea of following Jesus in servanthood impact you when you apply it in everyday circumstances?

Lie #20: I Need to Be Good So That God Will Love Me

1. In what ways do you try to earn God's love?
2. How would it feel to let go of your striving and accept God's love as a free gift?
3. How does the truth that you can't earn God's love change your view of how he feels about you?

Lie #21: I Don't Need to Change

1. What is one thing you would like to change in your life?
2. How has God brought about change in your life in the past?
3. How does knowing the truth that the Holy Spirit actually can bring about change in your life make you view your life?

Lie #22: I Don't Need People

1. In what areas of your life do you flaunt the "I can do it myself" attitude?

2. What part do you think you are in the body of Christ?
3. How do you use your life to benefit other believers?
4. In what ways is the truth that you need people in order to become the person you were designed to be evident in your life?

Lie #23: I Am Never Going to Get Free

1. What do you want to be free from?
2. What would being free look like to you?
3. What would being free feel like to you?
4. How does the truth that the man from Gerasenes sat in peace at the feet of Jesus after being tormented for years impact you and your longing to be free?

Susanna Foth Aughtmon is a pastor's wife and mother of three. She graduated from Bethany University with a BA in social science emphasizing psychology and early childhood education. After pursuing various careers, including teaching preschoolers and starting her own home interiors business, she decided to stay home as a full-time mom. She assists her husband, Scott, in various ministries at their church plant, Pathway Church, in Palo Alto, California.

Escape the Pressure to Be Perfect

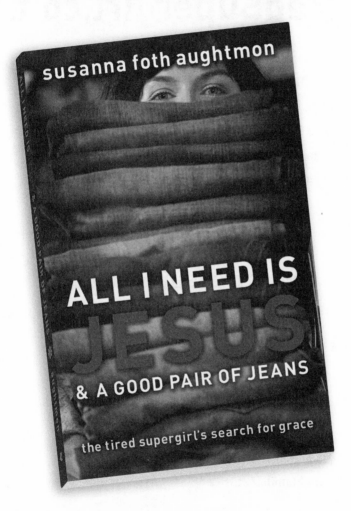

susanna foth aughtmon

ALL I NEED IS
JESUS
& A GOOD PAIR OF JEANS

the tired supergirl's search for grace

"Always with humor and style, Susanna captures
the beauty of following Jesus."
—Sara Groves, singer/songwriter

Revell
a division of Baker Publishing Group
www.RevellBooks.com

Available wherever books are sold.

Join the fun at
TiredSupergirl.com!

Calling all supergirls!

- Join in a conversation with other tsgs (tired supergirls)
- Sign up for the *Tired Supergirl Chronicles* newsletter
- Check out the latest tired supergirl sightings

All this and more at
www.tiredsupergirl.com

And check out Sue's blog,
Confessions of a Tired Supergirl,
at tiredsupergirl.blogspot.com
to meet Sue and read about her

- take on life as a mom of three boys, a church planter's wife, and a writer
- mishaps, cooking disasters, and other funny and familiar stories

See you there!